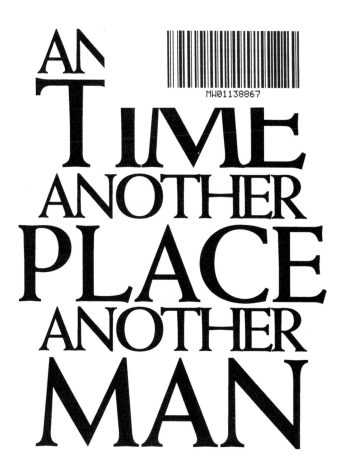

ANOTHER TIME ANOTHER PLACE ANOTHER MAN

A Biblical Alternative to the Traditional View of Creation

BASED ON THE WRITINGS OF

FINIS DAKE

**Edited by Mark Allison
and David Patton**

DAKE PUBLISHING

Unless otherwise noted, all Scripture quotations are from
the King James Version of the Bible.

Special thanks to Mike Janiczek for encouraging us to pursue
this project, and for his creative suggestion for the title.

Second Printing
March 2000

INTRODUCTION TO THE DAKE DOCTRINAL SERIES

Welcome to the first installment in a new series of books based on the writings of the late Finis Jennings Dake—the Dake Doctrinal Series!

Finis Dake was a man with unique gifts, not the least of which was his God-given ability to flawlessly quote Scripture—in perfect King James, including the punctuation! Yet he didn't allow this gift to take the place of diligent Bible study. On the contrary, in spite of his extensive teaching ministry and prolific writing career, Dake managed to spend over 100,000 hours immersed in the pages of Scripture. That's basically the equivalent of holding a full-time job for 50 years! And all the while he rigorously held to an early commitment to interpret the Bible literally wherever possible, and to teach nothing that he couldn't prove with two or three plain scriptures.

Such a single-minded devotion naturally affected his perspective on the Word of God and its teachings, giving him an outlook that often ran contrary to the status quo. As a result, there were times in Dake's life when he had little or no support for his views, and times when he was harshly opposed for leaving the safety of unchallenged dogmas to proclaim what he believed to be the simple truth of inspired Scripture.

Yet God blessed him as he persevered through these seasons of loneliness, and over the course of his life, many came to appreciate the genius of Dake's approach to the Bible.

Dake didn't write Christian fiction, and he didn't ride the waves of trendy topics. All of his vast writings were focussed on the somewhat narrow market of the serious Bible student. Unfortunately, that market has narrowed even further in the 35 years following the completion of *The Dake Annotated Reference Bible*. It's difficult these days in our fast-paced, stressed-out society to take the time we need to really study God's Word. Yet our need for such study is probably greater than it's ever been.

It is to help meet this need that we've introduced the Dake Doctrinal Series.

Since Dake's writings span virtually every subject in Scripture, they have something of a timeless quality. Yet the bulk of his work was written between the early 1930s and the late 1950s, and his style naturally reflects his era. It is thus the goal of the Dake Doctrinal Series to present key aspects of Dake's thought in a contemporary style. Though the words will often be those of the editors, it is our intent to remain true to the vision of Finis Jennings Dake.

David Patton
Director of Product Development
Dake Publishing, Inc.
January, 1997

Contents

Foreword

Another Time, Another Place, Another Man is dynamite and an answer for many people who are questioning these very issues. The answers that are presented are certainly scriptural and powerful.

All of my Christian life it seems like I have been involved in teaching some kind of home Bible studies. At the present time, our church is reaching out into our community with a lot of home Bible studies. Once a year I usually go to one of them and just do a question and answer time. I am astounded at the response and the questions of the people. They go right along with *Another Time, Another Place, Another Man*. How wonderful to have a book that you can put into their hands with Bible answers. These are intellectual people, they are people many times that are hungry, that have only been taught a cynical doctrine. It is good to have the truth to place before them, good for people to partake of life rather than death.

I thank God for this wonderful book.

Marilyn Hickey

Marilyn Hickey
Greenwood Village, Colorado
January 1997

Faith and science are locked in a battle for the hearts and minds of our generation. The war is waged perhaps most intensely in the classroom and on the campus, but the battle lines have been drawn and the conflict continues unabated in our homes, our workplaces and our churches.

It hasn't always been this way. Science was birthed out of the knowledge that God had created the universe with a logic and design that could be understood. Creation was a reflection of the Creator's personality, and to pursue an understanding of the things God had made was to inquire into the nature of God Himself. Thus, rather than facing each other in antagonistic opposition, faith and science traveled the same road, hand in hand.

Circumstances had changed by the mid-nineteenth century. When Darwin introduced _On the Origin of Species_ in the 1850's, Christians were quickly on the defensive, attempting to counter the claims of evolution with whatever weapons they could find at their disposal. Among the items in their arsenal was a theory mentioned in the writings of the early church fathers and which found its origins in Hebrew thought. If science was uncovering evidence for an earth millions, perhaps billions of years old—then this theory could provide some answers.

What had never really been openly debated suddenly became a controversial topic among theologians and academicians. If a gap did indeed exist in the creation account; if Genesis 1:1 did not flow directly into Genesis 1:2 as the next logical step in a continuous narrative, then a rethinking of the entire creation sequence was in order. On the other hand, the theory did provide room for a creation date pushed as far back into history as needed to allow for the unprecedented time spans required by contemporary scientific discoveries.

In the early part of the twentieth century, Finis Jennings Dake grappled with this theory and found substance in what had become nothing more than a weapon to fend off those seeking to undermine the literal interpretation of the Genesis creation account. Always requiring at least "two or three plain scriptures" upon which to base his interpretation of a biblical text, Dake found in the Bible a wealth of support for the existence of a pre-Adamite world.

As relevant in our day as it was in his, this *biblical* alternative to the traditional view of creation (the view that many of us have grown up with) is based on the writings of Finis Dake. Collected primarily from his seminal work *God's Plan for Man* and excerpts from the notes found in *The Dake Annotated Reference Bible*, the material in this book is essentially Dake's thought, albeit presented in a contemporary style.

It's our prayer that *Another Time . . . Another Place . . . Another Man* will speak to the issue of faith and science in a way that will bring both back to where they were intended by God to be — walking hand in hand.

Mark Allison, Editor
Dake Publishing, Inc.
January, 1997

Part One

DEFINITION
AND
DEFENSE

IN THE BEGINNING

Long before a man called Adam walked with God in the gardens of Eden, longer still before the flood of Noah covered the face of the earth, in a time called "the beginning," God created the heavens and the earth. A grand and beautiful design, the earth as conceived by the Creator was an exquisite home for the creatures He had fashioned. The earth itself was a magnificent garden where life flourished in a dazzling display of variety. The ground trembled with the footsteps of the largest creatures (those we now call dinosaurs). Animals filled the trees, the skies and the oceans. From eternity God had planned this creation, and it was perfect in every way. God created men and they began to settle in villages, cities and nations. Angels, a part of this new creation, were given dominion over the earth, to rule with the authority of their Creator. It was the archangel Lucifer who ruled over the nations in all the splendor of the greatest of God's creations. Every creature fashioned by the hand of God acted in perfect obedience to the will of their Creator. Angels and men knew God as a friend and drew their life from Him. There was no sickness or disease, no hunger or death, for there was no sin —

— Until Lucifer, the closest to the throne of God, the archangel who "walked up and down in the midst of the stones of fire," let the seed of pride find fertile ground in his heart. Pride led to rebellion, and rebellion to judgment. Lucifer and the nations following him were placed under a curse, and the earth itself was judged for their sin.

All of this happened before Genesis 1:2.

Not the Traditional View

Granted, this is not the traditional view of creation. Many may find it puzzling, perhaps even disturbing. Most of us who have been raised in the church have accepted the first two chapters of Genesis as a continuous, uninterrupted account of the origin of the earth and man. After all, many may argue, doesn't the book of Genesis make it perfectly clear that, in the beginning, God created the earth as a lifeless, shapeless, chaotic mass? Isn't it apparent, from the second verse of chapter one, that floods covered the earth while God's

Spirit hovered over what would become a beautiful new planet? Doesn't Scripture plainly record
the six days of creation and all that was involved
in forming the earth during that first week?

Before answering any of these questions,
it must be made clear that nothing will be presented in this book that is out of harmony with
God's Word. Every argument will be backed up
by biblical evidence, and no new ideas will be
submitted without the support of at least two or
three clear scriptural references. With that in
mind, let's take a look at what the Scriptures have
to say about the earth's origins.

The Clash With Science

It is generally acknowledged, based on
chronologies found in the Old Testament, that
Adam was created about 6,000 years ago, or about
4,000 B.C. Since Darwin published *The Origin of
the Species* in the mid-1800's, those who have held
to a literal interpretation of the Bible have
struggled to counter the claims of science for a
creation date stretching billions of years into the
past. Most of the scientific evidence accumulated
during the past century has supported these claims
of an old earth. Some argue that scientists are
basing their findings on previously-held assumptions relating to the earth's antiquity, that they are
merely seeing what they want to see. In other
words, they believe the evolutionary model which
requires an earth millions, perhaps billions of years

old, and interpret any evidence they find based on those assumptions. While there may be some merit to this, the fact remains that at best it is very difficult to explain much of the scientific evidence accumulated during the past century in light of a 6,000-year-old earth.

Unfortunately, this leaves the Christian with a dilemma. On the one hand, science claims the earth is billions of years old. On the other hand, biblical chronologies suggest that the earth is only about 6,000 years old. Faced with this tension between science and faith, the believer has two alternatives. One must either accept the scientific evidence and view the biblical creation account as mythology, or be forced to hold fast to a literal interpretation of the Scriptures and reject what science has to offer.

Neither of these alternatives are acceptable. The first violates basic exegetical principles. Nowhere in Scripture are we led to believe that either the recorded chronologies or the creation account are myths or allegories. Both the context and the language itself point to a literal interpretation. In fact, New Testament writers, inspired by the Holy Spirit, viewed the creation account as a literal event which took place at a specific point in history.

The second alternative requires the believer to "stick his head in the sand" and ignore the accumulated scientific evidence pointing to an old earth. As the weight of the evidence grows, the Christian must close his eyes all the more tightly to keep his faith intact. Not only is this unacceptable, it is unnecessary, as we'll soon see.

Maybe you haven't thought deeply about the subject because you were afraid that to do so might shake the foundation upon which your faith is built. Perhaps you've already been challenged in this area as a Christian in a secular society. If you're a parent, you may have been forced to wrestle with these issues as your children grapple with the evolutionary model being taught in our public schools.

Challenging the Common Assumption

Whether one accepts the scientific evidence or holds to a literal interpretation of the Bible, there is one point on which both camps agree: the Scriptures, literally interpreted, point to a creation date 6,000 years ago. This assumption is taken for granted in the debate between the two sides. It's accepted without question.

We don't agree. The entire premise of this book is that you can take the Genesis account very literally and not have any difficulty reconciling faith and science. We're going to challenge assumptions that both believers and nonbelievers have made for years. This isn't a two-sided issue, although that's traditionally the way it has been presented. Those who have sought answers to the question of the earth's origins have been puzzled by the apparent contradictions. There's a reason for that—a piece of the puzzle has been missing. Well, perhaps "misplaced" is a better word. You see, it's been there all along but we haven't known where to find it. The piece fits between Genesis 1:1 and 1:2 and we're going to take a look at it in the following chapters.

Chapter 2

CREATIONIST THEORIES

For more than a century Christians have grappled with the problem of science's claim for an old earth and the Bible's apparent demand for a creation date of around 4,000 B.C. The effort to reconcile science and Scripture has proceeded along separate lines. The gap theory and the day-age theory tackle the problem by trying to harmonize Scripture and science. The young earth theory views science as largely antagonistic to the claims of Scripture and, to a large degree, rejects any scientific data that might contradict God's Word. Theistic evolution takes the opposite approach and dismisses a literal interpretation of the Bible in order to accommodate scientific data.

In the following sections, we'll take a look at these theories and see what they have to offer the student of Scripture who is looking for a biblical solution to the creation/science controversy.

THE YOUNG EARTH THEORY

The young earth theory teaches that the earth was created about 6,000 years ago. This belief is based on genealogical records found in the Old Testament. Each creation day was a 24-hour period, and there was no gap between Genesis 1:1 and 1:2. Accordingly, scientific evidence pointing to an earth billions of years old is either dismissed as evolutionist propaganda, or refuted on the basis of a prior presumption that the earth is only 6,000 years old.

Proponents of the young earth theory believe that Noah's flood can account for the cataclysmic changes in the earth's surface. Thus, geological formations such as the Grand Canyon were not formed by gradual erosion from the Colorado River's passage, but by the receding floodwaters of Noah's time.

In support of the young earth theory, many Christian theorists have suggested that a vapor canopy circled the earth prior to the flood of Noah's day. Scriptural evidence to support this view is found in Genesis 2:4-6 which says that

> the LORD God made . . . every plant of the field before it was in the earth, and every herb of the field before it grew: for the LORD God

had not caused it to rain upon the earth, and
there was not a man to till the ground. But
there went up a mist from the earth, and watered the whole face of the ground.

It is suggested that this vapor canopy kept harm-
ful radiation from the earth's surface, which resulted in the long lifespans recorded prior to the
flood. It is further suggested that the fall of this
canopy, together with the opening of the "fountains of the deep" (Gen. 7:2), resulted in the flood
of Noah's day.

Young earth theorists believe that man and
dinosaur lived together (as indicated by passages
such as Job 41:1; 40:15), and that dinosaurs were
probably brought aboard the ark by Noah. Dinosaurs died out quickly following the flood, most
likely because of the change in climate and increased solar radiation resulting from the fall of
the canopy. Scripture speaks of God making "a
wind to pass over the earth" (Gen. 7:1), which
helped remove the floodwaters. Many young earth
creationists believe that the cooling brought about
by these evaporating waters caused the Ice Age.

Strengths and Weaknesses

This theory has a number of strengths, the
foremost of which is a strict adherence to a literal
translation of the text. The extremely long
lifespans recorded in Genesis are accounted for
by the presence of a vapor canopy, as is the ex-

tinction of the dinosaur population through increased solar radiation following the canopy's collapse. However, there are a few areas in which this theory falls short. While acknowledging the fact that the Bible plainly states that the six days of creation were literal days, young earth creationists fail to see the relevance of texts throughout Scripture which indicate a cataclysmic event of even greater proportions than Noah's flood. Proponents of this view reject scientific evidence which seems to indicate an earth much older than 6,000 years, even when to do so would appear extreme.

A God Who Deceives?

Many young earth creationists believe that God created the earth with the appearance of age. He placed fossils in the ground and fashioned geological formations to appear ancient. Obviously, this explanation carries with it an unsavory flavor of deception, as if God were trying to "fool" men into believing that the earth is indeed millions of years old. This idea of a deceiving God clearly contradicts Scripture. The Apostle Paul states that:

> the invisible things of him from the creation
> of the world are clearly seen, being under-
> stood by the things that are made, even his
> eternal power and Godhead; so that they are
> without excuse. (Rom. 1:20)

We can thus understand the "invisible things" of God by seeing the "things that are made." God would not have designed the earth with a deceptive appearance, unless it were in God's character to deceive. But we know from Titus that "God cannot lie" (Titus 1:2). Therefore, we know that God could not have created the earth to appear older than it is.

Scientific Problems

Why do we see light from stars that are millions of light-years away? If the universe was created 6,000 years ago, light from distant stars would not reach our planet for millions of years. In response, many holding to a young earth view believe that the speed of light has not always been a constant, and claim Einstein's Theory of Relativity to be flawed. Likewise, Radiocarbon and other dating systems are attacked on the grounds that levels of decay have fluctuated, or that radioactive isotopes formed as a byproduct of the decay process were present to begin with in the original material.

THE DAY-AGE THEORY

"But, beloved, be not ignorant of this one thing, that one day is with the Lord as a thousand years, and a thousand years as one day." So states the apostle in 2 Peter 3:8. Based on this text, the day-age theory is an attempt to reconcile scientific findings with God's Word. If the earth is indeed many thousands — perhaps even millions or billions — of years old, this theory can accommodate extended time frames within the limits set for us by Scripture.

According to this view, the creation of the earth and everything in it occurred in the order indicated in the Genesis account, with each "day" representing an age or time period of unknown duration. The day-age theory is incorporated as an element in the theory of progressive creationism, which claims that creation took place over an extended period of time, in an almost evolutionary manner. Contrary to the Darwinian model, progressive creationism sees God supernaturally creating new forms of life throughout the geologic ages. These new life forms were not a product of random mutation, as in the Darwinian model, but the result of God's progressive and orderly intervention in the process of creation.

The strength of both the day-age theory and progressive creationism is that they attempt to reconcile Scripture with the long time frames needed for an old earth. Unfortunately, both theories fall short of the mark when held up to the light of God's Word.

Proof of Literal Days

The Bible makes it very clear that the 6 days described in the first chapter of Genesis were literal 24-hour days, just as they have been ever since. The word "evening" in Genesis 1:5 is from the Hebrew `ereb*, meaning dusk, evening or night. It occurs at least 137 times, most often translated "evening" or its shortened form "even." It is consistently used in a literal sense outside of the creation material, so there is no reason to view it otherwise in the context of Genesis 1.

The word "morning" is literal as well. It comes from the Hebrew *boqer*, meaning dawn, break of day, morning or early light. *Boqer* is translated "morning" 190 times, and, like `ereb* above, is consistently literal outside the creation narrative, so there is no basis for treating it figuratively here.

It is true that the word "day" may refer to a prolonged period when it is qualified as "the day of the Lord." However, when it is used with words like "evening" and "morning," it can only be understood in the literal sense. Further emphasis is given to the literal meaning of the text by numbering each day as first, second, third, etc., as one naturally would number literal days. The context thus proves that the "day" and "night" here are literal days and nights, normal periods of light and darkness regulated by the sun, moon and stars, as mentioned elsewhere in Scripture (Gen. 8:22; Ps. 19:2; Job 38:12; Jer. 31:35-37; 33:19-26).

When the sabbath laws were given, God said "Six days shalt thou labour . . . For in six days the Lord made heaven and earth" (Ex. 20:8-11; 31:14-17). In other words, man was told to work the same length of time that it took to do the work of Genesis 1:3 - 2:25. It would be just as logical to argue that man was supposed to work 6,000 years or 6 indefinite periods of time before resting, as to argue that the days mentioned in the first chapter of Genesis were indefinite periods of time. It is never argued that the 6 days of Exodus 20 are long periods of time, yet they lack the clear qualifying terms found in Genesis 1.

A fundamental principle of biblical interpretation is to take Scripture literally when it is at all possible to do so. When the language cannot be interpreted in a literal manner, or when the text itself makes statements to the contrary, then the passage may be understood as having a figurative interpretation. On this basis we have to see the days in Genesis as literal, 24-hour days. Could not God do this work in 6 days as well as in 6,000 years? If He could, and if Scripture clearly states that He did, then we must accept a literal interpretation of the text.

Logical Problems

The day-age theory is not supported on a "commonsense" level. If this theory is true, then the waters remained on the earth at least 1,000 years before they were divided; the earth was still desolate another 1,000 years before vegetation was planted; and vegetation had to survive on earth 1,000 years before the sun, moon, and stars were created (if, as supposed, they were created on the fourth day).

Furthermore, we are told in Genesis 2:7-25 that man was created before the animals, and the animals were all created before the woman. In other words, Adam was created at the beginning and the woman at the end of the sixth day. If this day lasted for 1,000 years, then Adam would have been nearly 1,000 years old before a wife was made for him. Furthermore, God would have rested another 1,000 years between the making of Eve and the fall of man; so there would be about 2,000 years between Adam's creation and his fall. And yet, according to Genesis 5:1-3, Adam was only 130 years old when Seth was born.

It is true that some translations read "age" instead of "day," but that is a rare use of the Hebrew word (see "year" in Ex. 13:10), and this context doesn't support it. Even if "age" is a legitimate translation, an age can be any period of time, whether long or short. A 24-hour day *is* an age, albeit a short one.

The bottom line is that all the evidence points to literal days in the Genesis material, and the day-age theory fails to harmonize with this evidence.

THEISTIC EVOLUTION

A *Question of Authority*

The theories mentioned above all have at least one thing in common—they make Scripture the final authority on the subject of creation. All the claims of science are held up to the light of Scripture, and truth is only found when science can be understood and explained within a scriptural framework.

On the other hand, theistic evolution denies a literal interpretation of the Genesis creation account. According to this theory, man was not created from the dust of the earth, but evolved from lower forms of life following an evolutionary model. The primary difference between theistic evolution and Darwinian evolution is that in the former God controlled all the evolutionary processes.

A Biblically Unacceptable View

This theory violates one of the fundamental principles of biblical interpretation, which is to gather from the Scriptures themselves the precise meaning that the writers intended to convey. This process dictates that we must take the Bible literally wherever it is at all possible to do so. When the language cannot be taken literally, then we know it is figurative. We must then find the literal truth conveyed by the figurative language.

Unlike the other theories we have examined, theistic evolution subjects Scripture to scientific scrutiny and when found lacking, Scripture is then modified in order to harmonize with science. The end result is that theistic evolution allows man's wisdom to take precedence over the plain teachings of Scripture.

It is difficult to reconcile evolutionary theories with the Bible, and though proponents of theistic evolution attempt to do just that, they cannot interpret the Genesis account literally. It is impossible, for example, to claim that man evolved from lower life forms and still hold fast to the biblical account which speaks of God forming man and other living creatures out of the dust of the ground. Genesis 2:7 gives a detailed description of the creation of Adam. The language used here is very straightforward and not at all allegorical; the historical context of this passage gives us no other choice than to treat it as a literal account of the creation of man: "And the LORD God formed man of the dust of the ground, and breathed into his nostrils the breath of life; and man became a living soul" (Gen. 2:7).

Thus we see that Scripture clearly indicates that man's creation was not the byproduct of an evolutionary process, but the result of God's direct creative act at a specific point in history.

THE GAP THEORY

A Knee-Jerk Reaction?

Critics argue that the gap theory lacks a firm place in church tradition. They maintain that the biblical writers never speak plainly about what would be a significant event in earth's history. Many claim that the gap theory (so-called because of the apparent "gap" between Genesis 1:1 and 1:2) is simply a reaction to the evolutionist's demand for an earth billions of years old.

It is widely held that Scottish theologian Thomas Chalmers was the first to point to scriptural evidence for the possible existence of a pre-Adamite world. This interpretation of the creation account increased in popularity among Christians 45 years later when Darwin published his *On the Origin of Species* in 1859. For many, the gap theory provided a practical, biblical answer to the new scientific findings pointing to an "old earth," with a creation date pushed back millions of years. Because the gap theory was tied so closely to the early debate between creationists and evolutionists, many assumed that it was merely a last-ditch effort to find a solution to a dangerous attack on the veracity of Scripture.

Historical Foundations

However, we know that at least as early as the first century it was believed that a gap existed between the first two verses of Genesis. This interpretation of the Genesis account is also found in Jewish commentaries dating back to the Babylonian captivity. Noted Hebrew scholar Arthur Custance elaborates on the historicity of this view in his book *Without Form and Void*:

> A few of the early Church Fathers accepted this interpretation and based some of their

doctrines upon it. . . . The truth is, as we shall see, that the idea of a once ordered world having been brought to ruin as a consequence of divine judgment just prior to the creation of Adam, was apparently quite widespread. It was not *debated*: it was merely held by some and not by others. Those who held it referred to it and built up arguments upon it without apparently feeling the need to apologize for believing as they did, nor for explaining the grounds for their faith. During succeeding centuries not a few scholars kept the view alive, and medieval scholars wrote about it at some length — often using phraseology which gives their work a remarkably modern ring. And for the past two hundred years many translators and commentators have maintained the view and elaborated upon it at length. In short, it is not a recent interpretation of the text in Gen.1.1 and 1.2, but an ancient one long antedating modern geological views. Indeed — it could be as old as the writing of Gen.1.2 itself![1]

Custance notes that the earliest Aramaic translation of the Old Testament, the Targum of Onkelos, gives the following interpretation for Genesis 1:2: "and the earth was laid waste." This rendering clearly indicates that the Jewish scholars compiling one of the first translations of the Scriptures believed something happened between the first two verses of Genesis 1 which resulted in

1. Arthur C. Custance, *Without Form and Void* (Brockville, Ontario: Doorway Publications, 1970), 12.

the destruction of the original creation.[2] In the chapters that follow, we will explore in detail the textual basis for the gap theory.

2. Ibid., 14-15.

WITHOUT FORM AND VOID

To this point all we've really done is hurl a few questions at the traditional view of creation. At most, we've slightly cracked the foundations of commonly held beliefs about the age of the earth and the interpretation of the Genesis account. Now it's time to drive in a wedge and pry hard.

We'll do that by closely examining Genesis 1:2. The verse begins, "And the earth was without form, and void." What exactly does this mean? It sounds so ambiguous that we tend to just read it and go on without really thinking about it. Both the generally accepted interpretation and the most commonly used translations make this very easy to do. There are times, however, when it's wise to remember that if the majority were always right, the children of Israel would never have made it out of Egypt.

Ambiguity of the Traditional View

According to the traditional understanding of the passage, the description is that of some amorphous mass, awaiting the hand of the Creator to give it definition. The language used in most translations supports this idea. And because our minds aren't really trained to think this abstractly, we naturally don't expend a great deal of mental energy trying to do so. After all, if we accept the traditional view of this text, we're really trying to force our brains to supply definition to something that, by definition, lacks definition. If we carefully explore the original language of this text, however, we'll discover that the traditional view itself is "without form, and void."

The Hebrew Argument: Tohuw va Bohuw

The Hebrew word *tohuw*, rendered "without form" in the King James Version (KJV), occurs 19 times in the Old Testament. Its root idea is that of emptiness or waste. In a somewhat figurative sense, *tohuw* refers to empty or vain thoughts and pursuits. After God granted Israel's wicked desire to have a king, the prophet Samuel cautioned the people not to turn aside from following the Lord, but to serve Him with all of their heart (1 Sam. 12:20). If they did forsake the Lord, Samuel warned, they would then pursue "vain [*tohuw*] things, which cannot profit or deliver; for they are vain [*tohuw*]" (1 Sam. 12:21).

Isaiah displays a particular fondness for the

descriptive power of *tohuw*, using it eleven times. A characteristic of the wicked, according to this prophet, is their willingness to "turn aside the just for a thing of nought [*tohuw*]" (Isa. 29:21). Describing God's majesty and power, Isaiah says that "all nations before Him are as nothing; and they are counted to Him less than nothing, and vanity [*tohuw*]" (Isa. 40:17). A few verses later, the prophet says that God makes "the judges of the earth as vanity [*tohuw*]" (Isa. 40:23). Isaiah again translates *tohuw* as "vanity" when describing idolatry in 44:9.

In a physical sense (which is how it's used in Genesis 1:2), *tohuw* conveys the idea of barrenness or desolation. In Deuteronomy 32:10, Moses writes that God found Jacob "in a desert land" which he says was a "waste [*tohuw*] howling wilderness," or as the New International Version (NIV) translates it, "a barren and howling waste." Envisioning Jerusalem in the time of the future great tribulation, Isaiah refers to it as "the city of confusion (*tohuw*)" which he further describes as "broken down: every house is shut up that no man may come in" (Isa. 24:10). In Isaiah 34:11, the prophet describes the effects of Armageddon on the surrounding land with the words "confusion" (*tohuw*) and "emptiness." It is significant that the word "emptiness" here is the Hebrew word *bohuw*, translated "void" in Genesis 1:2. Its only other occurrence in Scripture is in Jeremiah 4:23 where Jeremiah describes a remarkable vision which we'll discuss in greater detail later in this book. Using the same Hebrew expression—*tohuw va bohuw*—found in Genesis 1:2, Jeremiah says, "I beheld the earth, and lo, it was *without form and void*" (italics added).

Earth in Chaos

The point of all this is to paint an accurate picture of the condition of the earth as we find it in Genesis 1:2. Rather than being a formless mass lacking creative definition (as in the assumption of the traditional view), Moses is offering us a very graphic portrayal of barrenness, waste and desolation. It is not the pristine void that anxiously awaits the Creator's initial touch, but the tragic emptiness which follows an all-encompassing destruction. Contrary to the generally accepted idea that "without form, and void" represents the first stage in the earth's creation, the language more appropriately describes the aftermath of a devastating cataclysmic event.

The bottom line is that the real sense of *tohuw va bohuw* is about as far away from the ambiguity of the traditional view as it could be. The truth is, it's genuinely impossible to conceive of this phrase modifying any aspect of original creation at all. This is especially true when we consider the words of Solomon who said that "He has made everything beautiful in its time" (Eccl. 3:11, NIV), a statement which stands in stark contrast to the desolation described in Genesis 1:2.

Isaiah's Conundrum

It's time to drive the wedge in and pry a little harder. Turning again to Isaiah, the predominant user of *tohuw* in the Old Testament, we get further confirmation that Genesis 1:2 has nothing to do with original creation:

> For thus saith the LORD that created the heavens; God himself that formed the earth and made it; He hath established it, He created it not in vain, He formed it to be inhabited: I am the LORD; and there is none else. (Isa. 45:18)

The word "vain" here is the Hebrew word *tohuw*. In this verse, Isaiah states in no uncertain terms that God did *not* create the world *tohuw*. In short, Isaiah directly contradicts the traditional understanding of Genesis 1:1-2.

The Power of Bara'

What makes this text even more powerful is that it contains two other Hebrew words which are vital components in forming an accurate interpretation of the Genesis material. The Hebrew word translated "created" both times in the verse is *bara'*. It is the same word used in Genesis 1:1, "In the beginning God **created** the heaven and the earth." As we will demonstrate, the usage of *bara'* throughout the Old Testament indicates new or original creation, bringing things into existence without the use of pre-existing material.

Such an understanding of creation is expressed in Hebrews 11:3 which states that "through faith we understand that the worlds were framed by the word of God, so that things which are seen were not made of things which do appear." It seems then that the actual substance God used to create the material universe was His spoken word. Physical matter was the result of a spiritual utterance; the visible was fashioned from the invisible. For this reason Jesus is called "the Word" in John 1, the third verse of which states that "all things were made by him; and without him was not any thing made that was made." Hebrews 1:2-3 concurs, revealing that Jesus was the one by whom God "made the worlds"; it is Christ who upholds "all things by the word of his power."

Our other key Hebrew word is `asah, translated "made" in Isaiah 45:18. `Asah makes its first appearance in Genesis 1:7, "And God **made** the firmament." It would appear at first that `asah and bara' are synonymous or interchangeable, both referring to acts of creation. Usage will prove otherwise, however. Dr. Arthur Custance, to whom we have referred earlier, states that "it is often found that light is shed upon the fundamental meaning of a word by noting the way in which it is first used in Scripture."[1] With this principle in mind, a clear distinction emerges between bara' and `asah, a distinction which is both deepened and sustained throughout Scripture.

---

1. Custance, 178.

We will start by looking at the comparatively rare uses of *bara'*. This word is primarily used in two ways: first, with respect to the creation of the material universe; and second, with specific regard to the creation of man who is the unique focus of the Creator's attention.

In addition to its initial appearance regarding the original creation of the heavens and the earth in Genesis 1:1, *bara'* is used of the creation of sea creatures and fowl in 1:21, and of mankind a few verses later: "So God **created** man in his own image, in the image of God **created** he him; male and female **created** he them" (Gen. 1:27). *Bara'* is then used to summarize God's creative work in Genesis 2:3-4. It's only other uses in Genesis refer to God's creation of man. As such it is used in Genesis 5:1-2 to introduce the genealogies. Then in Genesis 6:7, *bara'* is used in a context of regret: "And the LORD said, I will destroy man whom I have **created** from the face of the earth." It is used again of man's creation in Deuteronomy 4:32. In Psalm 51:10 David offers his famous prayer, "**Create** in me a clean heart, O God." Ethan the Ezrahite uses *bara'* to express God's creative sovereignty:

> The heavens are thine, the earth also is thine: as for the world and the fulness thereof, thou hast founded them. The north and the south thou hast **created** them: Tabor and Hermon shall rejoice in thy name. (Ps. 89:11-12)

Near the end of that same Psalm, Ethan speaks of the seeming futility of man's existence: "Remember how short my time is: wherefore hast thou **made** all men in vain?" (Ps. 89:47). Future generations of men will also be created by God (Ps. 102:18). Indeed, every living thing owes its existence to God's creation (Ps. 104:30; 148:5). Consequently, Solomon the Preacher urges us, "Remember now thy **Creator** in the days of thy youth" (Eccl. 12:1). Likewise Isaiah exhorts,

> Lift your eyes and look to the heavens: who **created** all these? He who brings out the starry host one by one, and calls them each by name. Because of his great power and mighty strength, not one of them is missing. . . . The LORD is the everlasting God, the **Creator** of the ends of the earth. (Isa. 40:26-28, NIV)

In Isaiah 42:5, God is referred to as

> he that **created** the heavens, and stretched them out; he that spread forth the earth, and that which cometh out of it; he that giveth breath unto the people upon it, and spirit to them that walk therein.

In addition to the physical universe, God created the people of Israel (Isa. 43:1, 7, 15; Mal. 2:10) and man to populate the earth (Isa. 45:12). Even Lucifer himself was God's creation (Ezek. 28:13, 15).

The Nuances of `Asah

In contrast to *bara'*, which is found only 54 times in the entire Old Testament, `asah* is quite common, occurring over 2,600 times. As mentioned above, `asah* first appears in Genesis 1:7, "And God **made** the firmament." `Asah* lacks the creative power conveyed by *bara'*, as the surrounding context clearly reveals:

> And God said, Let there be a firmament in the midst of the waters, and let it divide the waters from the waters. And God made the firmament, and divided the waters which were under the firmament from the waters which were above the firmament: and it was so. And God called the firmament Heaven. (Gen. 1:6-8)

Appointment

Rather than creation out of nothing by the raw power of God's spoken word, the idea here is that of appointment. The firmament was appointed to its specific task of dividing waters. Beyond that, it is the place where the heavenly bodies are set (vv. 14-18). So it appears atmospheric when directly related to earth (separating oceans from clouds), but it expands to include outer space itself, containing the sun, moon and stars. (Indeed, the NIV offers "expanse" as the translation of the Hebrew word for firmament.) Yet God had already *created* the heavens and the earth (v. 1).

The concept of appointment is further

emphasized when we encounter `asah again:

> And God **made** two great lights; the greater
> light to rule the day, and the lesser light to
> rule the night: he made the stars also. And
> God set them in the firmament of the heaven
> to give light upon the earth, and to rule over
> the day and over the night, and to divide the
> light from the darkness: and God saw that it
> was good. (Gen. 1:16-18)

Now, God had already said, "Let there be light,"
and He had already "divided the light from the
darkness," distinguishing night and day (Gen. 1:3-
5). Therefore, Genesis 1:16-18 does not reveal the
creation of the sun, moon and stars, but rather
their *appointment* to specific tasks.

Appointment is thus one of the founda-
tional meanings of `asah, as is abundantly clear
in several texts where it is used. In his rebellion,
Jeroboam "**made** priests of the lowest of the
people" (1 Ki. 12:31). When David was pretend-
ing allegiance to Achish the Philistine, it is recorded that

> In those days the Philistines gathered their
> forces to fight against Israel. Achish said to
> David, "You must understand that you and
> your men will accompany me in the army."
>
> David said, "Then you will see for yourself
> what your servant can do."
>
> Achish replied, "Very well, I will **make** you
> my bodyguard for life." (1 Sam. 28:1-2, NIV)

Though the concept of appointment is obvious in these passages, it isn't difficult to see in God's covenant promise to Abram when He said, "I will **make** of thee a great nation" (Gen. 12:2; cf. Ex. 32:10). Similarly, if Israel would keep His commandments, God promised to **make** them "high above all nations" (Dt. 26:19). It was further promised them, "And the LORD shall **make** thee the head, and not the tail" (Dt. 28:13). By way of encouragement, Samuel told Israel, "it hath pleased the LORD to **make** you his people" (1 Sam. 12:22). One of the rewards for the man who killed Goliath was that Saul promised to "**make** his father's house free in Israel" (1 Sam. 17:25).

Accomplishment

Appointment isn't the only meaning of `asah*, however. Most often translated by forms of "do," `asah* expresses the idea of accomplishment as well. When God confronted Eve for her sin, He asked, "What is this that thou hast **done**?" (Gen. 3:13). Then He charged the serpent, saying, "Because thou hast **done** this, thou art cursed" (Gen. 3:14). At the zenith of blatant ambition, the planning committee for the tower of Babel said, "let us **make** us a name" (Gen. 11:4).

Creativity

Accomplishment naturally lends itself to the creative ability expressed by the word "make"—hence, the ease with which `asah* refer-

ences in Genesis 1-2 have been traditionally mis-
construed as acts of original creation. Implying
the first animal sacrifice, we see God "**make** coats
of skin" (Gen. 3:21). Later He commanded Noah,
"**Make** thee an ark" (Gen. 6:14). Israel frequently
violated the second commandment, "Thou shalt
not **make** unto thee any graven image" (Ex. 20:4).
And `asah was used extensively in the instructions
for things Israel was to **make** for the tabernacle
and related worship (Ex. 25-30).

It is in this latter sense that "God **made** the
beast of the earth" (Gen. 1:25). And though man
was uniquely created (*bara'*, Gen. 1:27, etc.), God
also "formed man of the dust of the ground" (Gen.
2:7). Consequently, the Trinity conferred together,
"Let us **make** man in our image" (Gen. 1:26).

The Argument From Isaiah

We can see, then, in the abundant uses of
`asah, there is nothing that truly approaches the
sheer creative energy expressed by *bara'*. With
bara', we have created substance appearing where
no substance existed before. `Asah, on the other
hand, denotes that which is made out of pre-existing materials. Having demonstrated this, we're
able now to meaningfully interpret Isaiah 45:18
in light of its significance for the Genesis account:

> For thus saith the LORD that created [*bara'*]
> the heavens; God himself that formed the
> earth and made [`asah] it; He hath established

it, He created [*bara'*] it not in vain [*tohuw*],
He formed it to be inhabited: I am the LORD;
and there is none else. (Isa. 45:18)

Understanding now that *bara'* refers to original
creation, we can see clearly that God did not originally create the earth "in vain," or "without form"
as it is described in Genesis 1:2. Hence, we have
further proof that Genesis 1:2 does not refer to
the first stage of original creation, but is rather
the aftermath of vast destruction.

If this is true, as we believe it is, then we
have a mystery on our hands. If "without form,
and void" does not describe God's original creation of the earth, something must have happened
to produce these results. The answer to that question will be given in the next chapter. For now,
however, let's return to Genesis 1:2 and confirm
that we're on the right track.

Widening the Gap

Once again, another Hebrew word helps
complete the puzzle. This time it's the easily overlooked verb: "And the earth **was** without form,
and void." The Hebrew word *hayah* is richer than
the simple "was" would imply. More than just a
state of being, *hayah* suggests the process of *becoming*.

This understanding is clear from at least
134 places where the King James translators cor-
rectly rendered this sense of *hayah*. A few ex-

amples will suffice, however. It was after God breathed into Adam the breath of life that "man **became** a living soul" (Gen. 2:7). When Lot's wife looked back on the destruction of Sodom and Gomorrah, "she **became** a pillar of salt" (Gen. 19:26). When Moses obediently cast his rod on the ground, "it **became** a serpent"; when he picked it up, "it **became** a rod in his hand" (Ex. 4:3-4). After Saul prophesied in fulfillment of Samuel's prediction, "it **became** a proverb, Is Saul also among the prophets?" (1 Sam. 10:12).

In each of these passages (and many others), *hayah* clearly indicates a state of becoming that is the result of some type of cause-and-effect relationship. The same is true in Genesis 1:2. The earth *became* without form and void. But, as Isaiah states, it wasn't created that way "in the beginning." Hence, there appears to be a gap between Genesis 1:1 and 1:2. In the next chapter we will look at some of the events that fill this gap.

THE FALL OF LUCIFER

We've established that the chaotic state of
the earth as we find it in Genesis 1:2 could not
possibly reflect the early stages of creation. On
the contrary, a careful study of the original language demands that we understand this pivotal
verse as descriptive of a cataclysmic desolation,
the aftermath of a global catastrophe. These conditions clash with everything we have traditionally believed about the Genesis account, forcing
us to wonder how this verse could possibly relate
to the original creation of the heavens and the
earth. Isaiah further confirms the validity of such
questions by clearly stating that God did *not* create the world to look as it does in Genesis 1:2.
Hence, we are compelled to consider a gap of
unspecified time between the original creation

"in the beginning," and an earth "without form, and void." The major events which fill that gap are the subject of this chapter.

Long before Adam roamed Eden, sin had already found root in the heart of another. From his first appearance in the pages of Scripture, we find Lucifer intent on man's destruction. Hating the innocence of earth's new rulers, Lucifer used the serpent to tempt Eve in the garden:

> Now the serpent was more crafty than any of the wild animals the LORD God had made. He said to the woman, "Did God really say, 'You must not eat from any tree in the garden'?" The woman said to the serpent, "We may eat fruit from the trees in the garden, but God did say, 'You must not eat fruit from the tree that is in the middle of the garden, and you must not touch it, or you will die.'" "You will not surely die," the serpent said to the woman. (Gen. 3:1-4, NIV)

We all know how this story ends, for in one way or another we daily contend with the corruption it unleashed. But for the purposes of this study, we are struck by the fact that sin was present prior to Adam's appearance on the scene. When did it first appear? Obviously, Lucifer had already turned against God before the Creator reached down into the earth's clay to make man in His own image. Did evil itself peer over the shoulder of God during the six days of Genesis 1 as the

Creator pronounced each of His acts good and perfect? We'll find an answer to these questions as we look at Lucifer's fall and find the connection between his past and the history of the pre-Adamite world. And, as we look at the circumstances surrounding Lucifer's fall, it will become apparent that his rebellion is linked to the condition of the earth described in Genesis 1:2.

Lucifer's Earthly Kingdom

Several Old Testament passages speak of Lucifer's fall, but none give a comprehensive, detailed account of the historical context surrounding those events. On the other hand, there are many pieces to the puzzle embedded within certain prophetic messages that, when placed together, give us a vivid picture of the earth before sin touched the first heart.

Turning the pages of Isaiah, we find a prophecy concerning the king of Babylon in the fourteenth chapter. At first, the text is referred to as a "proverb against the king of Babylon" (Isa. 14:4). As we study this passage, however, we find several statements which cannot possibly be made of an earthly king. These verses are generally accepted as referring to the fall of Lucifer:

> How art thou fallen from heaven, O Lucifer, son of the morning! how art thou cut down to the ground, which didst weaken the nations! For thou hast said in thine heart, I will as-

cend into heaven, I will exalt my throne above
the stars of God: I will sit also upon the mount
of the congregation, in the sides of the north:
I will ascend above the heights of the clouds;
I will be like the most High. (Isa. 14:12-14)

The Hebrew word for Lucifer is *heylel*
which means "light-bearer." This is the only occurrence of the word in Scripture. Since he is
further characterized as the "son of the morning"
(Isa. 14:12), we have proof that he is no earthly
man. This is clearly an example of what is known
as the "law of double reference." We see this principle at work in passages of Scripture where both
a visible person, and an invisible person working
through that person, are addressed at the same
time. In most instances the invisible person is
using the visible person as a tool to hinder the
plan of God.

For example, when Jesus said to Peter, "Get
behind me, Satan! You are a stumbling block to
me; you do not have in mind the things of God,
but the things of men" (Mt. 16:23, NIV), Jesus
didn't mean that Peter himself was the devil, but
that he was being used as a tool of Satan to keep
Christ from getting to the cross. Hence, both Peter and Satan are addressed and involved in the
statement. To understand passages in which
double references are being made, one should
see the part of the passage that can refer to an
earthly person as doing so, and those parts that
cannot possibly refer to an earthly person as re-

ferring to the invisible person also addressed.

Through Isaiah's eyes we can peer down the corridor of time and see fragments of history that took place before Adam was formed. Angels walked the earth in the purity of holiness as each did the will of his Creator. Lucifer, an angel created by God, was given widespread authority and power. His position and influence were such that the archangels themselves were hesitant to confront Lucifer under their own authority. Jude states that

> even the archangel Michael, when he was disputing with the devil about the body of Moses, did not dare to bring a slanderous accusation against him, but said, "The Lord rebuke you!" (Jude 9, NIV)

It seems clear that Lucifer must have held a position of rulership second only to God Himself.

In this passage Isaiah portrays Lucifer's exalted status prior to his fall through rebellion. Writing under the inspiration of the Holy Spirit, Isaiah records that Lucifer had a throne, obviously signifying rulership or kingship. Likewise, rulership implies subjects to rule. Furthermore, since Lucifer was charged with weakening the nations, there must have been nations in existence for him to weaken. In the sense of a visible, personal rule on earth, Lucifer had no kingdom at the time of Adam's creation and hasn't had one since; he has only ruled through others since

Adam's day. Therefore, Isaiah's prophecy must refer to a time before Adam.

Isaiah declares that Lucifer's kingdom was on earth. "I will ascend above the heights of the clouds," Lucifer boasts in verse fourteen. How could he have attempted to ascend above the clouds and stars and into heaven itself if he already lived in heaven? Why would this kind of language be used, if not to emphasize Lucifer's earthly position prior to his rebellion against God?

It is apparent that Lucifer wasn't in heaven when he rebelled, or he wouldn't have determined to *ascend* into heaven. His kingdom had to have been located under the stars for him to want to be exalted above them. He was under the clouds, or he couldn't have desired to ascend above them.

Paul states in his letter to the church at Colossae that Christ has created thrones, dominions, principalities, and powers in heaven and on earth (Col. 1:16). Lucifer was evidently given authority along these lines over the earth and its inhabitants. In addition, the now-familiar text of Isaiah 45:18 proves that God created the earth to be inhabited by earthly creatures:

> For thus saith the LORD that created the heavens; God himself that formed the earth and made it; he hath established it, he created it not in vain, *he formed it to be inhabited*" (emphasis added).

Turn a few more pages until we reach the book of Ezekiel where we'll find additional information relating to Lucifer's rule during this pre-Adamite period. The prophet Ezekiel adds a few more pieces to the puzzle that Isaiah began to shape for us. Ezekiel expands the description of Lucifer's position and the cause of his rebellion. Once again, we have another example of the law of double reference. The earthly man addressed in this passage was the king of Tyre:

> This is what the Sovereign LORD says: "You were the model of perfection, full of wisdom and perfect in beauty. You were in Eden, the garden of God; every precious stone adorned you: ruby, topaz and emerald, chrysolite, onyx and jasper, sapphire, turquoise and beryl. Your settings and mountings were made of gold; on the day you were created they were prepared. You were anointed as a guardian cherub, for so I ordained you. You were on the holy mount of God; you walked among the fiery stones. You were blameless in your ways from the day you were created till wickedness was found in you. Through your widespread trade you were filled with violence, and you sinned. So I drove you in disgrace from the mount of God, and I expelled you, O guardian cherub, from among the fiery stones. Your heart became proud on account of your beauty, and you corrupted your wisdom because of your splendor. So I threw you to the earth; I made a spectacle of you before kings. By your many sins and dishonest trade you

have desecrated your sanctuaries. So I made
a fire come out from you, and it consumed
you, and I reduced you to ashes on the ground
in the sight of all who were watching. All the
nations who knew you are appalled at you;
you have come to a horrible end and will be
no more." (Ezek. 28:12-19, NIV)

Another Eden

The dwelling place of Lucifer was "Eden,
the garden of God." This was not a mere summer
residence of some earthly king of Tyre, but the
garden of God as referred to in other Old Testament passages. For example, we see Isaiah pro-
claiming the Lord's favor as he comforts Zion by
making "her wilderness like Eden, and her desert
like the garden of the LORD" (Isa. 51:3). Ezekiel
pronounces a prophecy against Pharaoh saying
"I have made him fair by the multitude of his
branches: so that all the trees of Eden, that were
in the garden of God, envied him" (Ezek. 31:9).
Prophesying concerning the Day of the Lord, Joel
proclaims:

> A fire devoureth before them; and behind
> them a flame burneth: the land is as the gar-
> den of Eden before them, and behind them
> a desolate wilderness; yea, and nothing shall
> escape them. (Joel 2:3)

The Eden described by Ezekiel, however,
was not the garden in which God placed Adam,
for in Adam's Eden, "every precious stone" was

not the covering of Satan, nor was he the perfect, sinless guardian cherub. Therefore, this must have been a pre-Adamite Eden, the garden that God made as the location of Lucifer's earthly kingdom, long before Adam walked the Eden of his day.

It is apparent that Lucifer was the ruler of this Eden, for the descriptive references used by both Isaiah and Ezekiel indicate authority and rulership over nations. We've already read in Isaiah of Lucifer's throne and the nations he weakened. Ezekiel completes the picture of the honor bestowed on absolute rulers with his vivid description of Lucifer being adorned with "every precious stone." Lucifer's authority is further noted in Ezekiel 28:14 where he is referred to as being "anointed as a guardian cherub." The King James Version renders this phrase, "the anointed cherub that covereth." The Hebrew word for "covereth" is *sakak*, meaning to entwine, fence in, protect, defend, or hedge in. The word is repeated in verse 16 where Lucifer is called the "covering cherub." Tracing *sakak* throughout the Old Testament, we see that it is used of the wings of the cherubim covering the mercy seat (Ex. 25:20; 37:9; 1 Ki. 8:7; 1 Chr. 28:18); of God covering (and thus protecting) Moses when His glory passed by (Ex. 33:22); of the ark being covered with the veil (Ex. 40:3, 21); of God defending those who trust in Him (Ps. 5:11); of the protective covering of God's wings over the one who abides in Him (Ps. 91:4); and of God covering David's head in battle (Ps.

140:7). This indicates that Lucifer was responsible for protecting and ruling over the Eden and mountain of God described in this passage.

The "mountain of God" found in Ezekiel 28:14 gives us further evidence that Lucifer's rule was on the earth itself. In every other passage where the Hebrew phrase *har Elohim* occurs, it refers to a literal, earthly mountain. In Exodus 3:1 it refers to Horeb, where Moses saw the burning bush. In Exodus 4:27 it was where Moses and Aaron met. Moses camped there in Exodus 18:5, and he climbed it to meet God in Exodus 24:13. It was where Elijah sought the Lord in 1 Kings 19:8. In every instance it is used in reference to a literal, earthly mountain (Ex. 3:1; 4:27; 18:5; 24:13; 1 Ki. 19:8; Ps. 69:15; Ezek. 28:16). The phrase *har Jehovah*, the "mount of the LORD," is also used in Scripture of an earthly mountain (Gen. 22:14; Num. 10:33; Ps. 24:3; Isa. 2:3; 30:29; Mic. 4:2; Zech. 8:3).

Lucifer's Rebellion

We have no direct statement in the Scriptures to precisely indicate the time frame for Lucifer's rebellion. On the other hand, we do have several good clues that point to a fall prior to the events which took place during creation week.

The first bit of evidence indicating a pre-Adamite rebellion is found in Isaiah 14. Here we see that one of the results of Lucifer's actions was to "weaken the nations." As we've said, these "nations" must have existed prior to the creation of Adam, for the context of the passage relates to the time of Lucifer's rebellion, not his present influence on Adam's race.

According to Isaiah, the ground, clouds, stars and heaven were already created before Lucifer's rebellion. And we've already seen that Lucifer's fall occurred before his temptation of Adam in the garden. Therefore, these events must have taken place on the earth, but before Adam was created. Even if this rebellion could have occurred during the six days of creation (though there appears to be no time for it), it is conspicuously absent from the creation narrative. Consequently, Lucifer *must* have rebelled prior to the six days of creation.

We don't know how long it took for the seed of rebellion to grow in the heart of Lucifer. Ezekiel tells us that Lucifer became filled with violence by his "widespread trade" (Ezek. 28:16). Two verses later the NIV refers to this as "dishonest trade," but the KJV seems to grasp the deeper moral implications with its translation, "the iniquity of thy traffick" (Ezek. 28:18). The root of the Hebrew word for "traffick" here is *rakal* which is consistently translated "merchant" in the KJV. It conveys the idea of traveling around, possibly suggesting the idea of going about as a slanderer in a moral sense. This image is certainly consistent with Satan's character as the accuser of the brethren (Rev. 12:10) and the father of lies (Jn. 8:44).

Apparently, Lucifer began to accuse God and led others to rebel with him. He may have stirred rebellion in the hearts of others for days, weeks, decades or centuries before he dared to lead a revolt into heaven. Ultimately, that rebellion involved not only the inhabitants of the pre-Adamite world, but Satan was so persuasive in his slanderous appeals that one-third of God's angels joined him in this futile effort to dethrone the King of kings (Rev. 12:4, 7-10).

We are told that Satan had "sanctuaries" which he defiled by his iniquities and slander (Ezek. 28:18). This suggests a long and bitter feud between God and Satan before God took action to remove him from his position and curse the earth. Satan was surely bitter in his slander of God and probably accused Him of being an unjust tyrant in His rule over creation. True to His unchanging character, God was no doubt longsuffering; but when the final invasion of heaven took place, we can only imagine how quickly and effortlessly God put down the rebellion.

Lucifer's Judgment

Lucifer is the only person in all of Scripture who is spoken of as falling from heaven. Obviously, he was cast back down to earth as a result of his failed attempt to usurp God's rule over the universe. According to Luke's faithful record,

And the seventy returned again with joy, saying, Lord, even the devils are subject unto us through thy name. And he said unto them, I beheld Satan as lightning fall from heaven. Behold, I give unto you power to tread on serpents and scorpions, and over all the power of the enemy: and nothing shall by any means hurt you. Notwithstanding in this rejoice not, that the spirits are subject unto you; but rather rejoice, because your names are written in heaven. (Lk. 10:17-20)

Ezekiel records the event from God's perspective:

Through your widespread trade you were filled with violence, and you sinned. So I drove you in disgrace from the mount of God, and I expelled you, O guardian cherub, from among the fiery stones. Your heart became proud on account of your beauty, and you corrupted your wisdom because of your splendor. So I threw you to the earth; I made a spectacle of you before kings. By your many sins and dishonest trade you have desecrated your sanctuaries. So I made a fire come out from you, and it consumed you, and I reduced you to ashes on the ground in the sight of all who were watching. (Ezek. 28:16-18, NIV)

Whereas the KJV renders a future tense, "I will cast thee as profane" and "I will cast thee to the ground," the NIV rightly translates the past tense of the original Hebrew here. These phrases must be understood in the past tense to harmonize with the rest of the passage which doesn't refer to the king who was reigning over Tyre in Ezekiel's day, but to the fall of Lucifer sometime in the dateless past, long before the six days of re-creation recorded in Genesis 1.

Not only was Lucifer cast down to the ground (as in Isaiah 14:12-14 and Luke 10:18), but he was also stripped of his position and glory, and removed from the mountain of God in the garden where he had his throne (Ezek. 28:14-19). He was thus thrown back to the earth in utter defeat and humiliation. Luke's reference to the defeat of Satan and his fall to earth "as lightning" corresponds to Ezekiel's description of fire coming out of him and his being reduced to "ashes on the ground." This is figurative of absolute defeat and humiliation. Satan will face even further judgment for his actions in the future tribulation, and will ultimately be put in the abyss at the second coming of Christ (Rev. 12:3-14; 19:11 - 20:3).

Reflections on Lucifer's Fall

Lucifer was the first of God's creation to exalt himself in pride, and he and his angelic followers were the first to attempt the overthrow of God's government. Had they remained true to God, Lucifer and those living under his rule would have continued to live on earth and carry out God's plan for His creation.

But Lucifer fell and led the earth into its first sinful state. With Adam's rebellion, the earth experienced the consequences of sin for the second time. It is God's plan to rid the earth of all

rebellion and to fully restore the universal kingdom of God where God is eternally "all in all."
Thus, the entire biblical message is centered
around the complete redemption of man. We can
see this clearly in Paul's letter to the church at
Corinth:

> Then cometh the end, when he shall have
> delivered up the kingdom to God, even the
> Father; when he shall have put down all rule
> and all authority and power. For he must
> reign, till he hath put all enemies under his
> feet. The last enemy that shall be destroyed is
> death. For he hath put all things under his
> feet. But when he saith all things are put un-
> der him, it is manifest that he is excepted,
> which did put all things under him. And when
> all things shall be subdued unto him, then
> shall the Son also himself be subject unto him
> that put all things under him, that God may
> be all in all. (1 Cor. 15:24-28)

In God's plan, we are now nearing the end
of Adam's rebellion. God is soon to send Christ
with the armies of heaven to defeat the armies of
the Antichrist and seize the governments of this
world. This He will do in one day, according to
the prophet Zechariah, for the purpose of setting
up a righteous government on earth forever: "But
it shall be one day which shall be known to the
LORD, not day, nor night: but it shall come to pass,
that at evening time it shall be light" (Zech. 14:7).
God's sovereignty will be restored in all

parts of the universe during the first 1,000 years of the eternal kingdom, as it was before both Lucifer and Adam rebelled. Saints, the redeemed ones of the human race from the time of Adam to the second coming of Christ, will eternally reign as kings and priests under God and Christ over the dominion originally given to Adam:

> LORD our Lord, how excellent is thy name in all the earth! who hast set thy glory above the heavens. Out of the mouth of babes and sucklings hast thou ordained strength because of thine enemies, that thou mightest still the enemy and the avenger. When I consider thy heavens, the work of thy fingers, the moon and the stars, which thou hast ordained; What is man, that thou art mindful of him? and the son of man, that thou visitest him? For thou hast made him a little lower than the angels, and hast crowned him with glory and honour. Thou madest him to have dominion over the works of thy hands; thou hast put all things under his feet: All sheep and oxen, yea, and the beasts of the field; The fowl of the air, and the fish of the sea, and whatsoever passeth through the paths of the seas. O LORD our Lord, how excellent is thy name in all the earth! (Ps. 8:1-9)

We can now put a few more pieces of the puzzle together. Aided by the words of Isaiah and Ezekiel, we've already seen that Lucifer had an earthly kingdom in which he ruled entire nations, long before Eve met the serpent in Eden. And we know that at some point, Lucifer weakened these nations, leading them and a third of God's angels in a rebellion which resulted in some kind of judgment. There is, therefore, an extensive history which is not detailed in the Genesis account. In addition, as we discovered in the previous chapter, there is a conspicuous gap between Genesis 1:1 and 1:2, a gap which could easily contain the entire rise and fall of the pre-Adamite civilization.

Finally, we are convinced that Lucifer's fall and subsequent judgment must have happened before God's creation of man in the first chapter of Genesis, for Adam and Eve clearly represent a pristine, sinless stage in earth's history. And while we don't have all the details of the pre-Adamite judgment, we do have a description of its aftermath in Genesis 1:2.

In the previous chapter we explored only the first line of Genesis 1:2, "and the earth was without form, and void." The rest of the verse, as it relates to the destruction of the pre-Adamite world, will be the focus of chapter five.

DARKNESS UPON THE FACE
OF THE DEEP

In the last chapter we established the fact that the archangel Lucifer ruled an earthly civilization prior to God's creation of Adam (hence the term "pre-Adamite"). He led these nations in his rebellion until God finally determined to destroy this world and start over. This entire history took place sometime after Genesis 1:1, with the aftermath of the judgment being described in Genesis 1:2. Having laid this foundation, we'll now return to Genesis 1:2 to examine the second half of the verse to see what it has to say about the destruction of the pre-Adamite world.

"And the earth was without form, and void; and darkness was upon the face of the deep. And the Spirit of God moved upon the face of the waters." The third chapter of this book was devoted to a rather thorough study of the phrase "without form, and void." We concluded that the original Hebrew, *tohuw va bohuw*, could not possibly describe the shapeless mass of the earth in its initial stages of creation, as the traditional interpretation of the text had long held. Rather, as usage of the original language dictated, we found ourselves looking at the barrenness and desolation of some global cataclysm which we now understand to have been the aftermath of the destruction of the pre-Adamite world.

DARKNESS IN SCRIPTURE

As we press on in Genesis 1:2, let us first explore the significance of the darkness which prevailed upon the earth. Though traditionally understood as the natural state of original creation prior to God's command, "Let there be light" (Gen. 1:3), we interpret the darkness of Genesis 1:2 as part of the judgment on the pre-Adamite world. Is this an arbitrary decision on our part, simply to support the rest of our argument? On the contrary, there is ample scriptural precedence for associating darkness and judgment.

Life Apart From God

Of course, the ultimate contrast between light and darkness centers around that which is of God and that which is not, for "God is light, and in him is no darkness at all" (1 Jn. 1:5). Jesus declared, "I am the light of the world: he that followeth me shall not walk in darkness, but shall have the light of life" (Jn. 8:12).

In this sense, darkness represents every aspect of life apart from God. In the introduction to his gospel, John writes of Jesus that "in him was life; and the life was the light of men. And the light shineth in the darkness; and the darkness comprehended it not" (Jn. 1:4-5).

The Darkness of Sin

Furthermore, darkness and light are incompatible. As Paul wrote to the Corinthians, "what communion hath light with darkness?" (2 Cor. 6:14). And in the Sermon on the Mount, Jesus cautioned, "but if thine eye be evil, thy whole body shall be full of darkness. If therefore the light that is in thee be darkness, how great is that darkness!" (Mt. 6:23; Lk. 11:34-35). Consequently,

> If we say that we have fellowship with him, and walk in darkness, we lie, and do not the truth: but if we walk in the light, as he is in the light, we have fellowship one with another, and the blood of Jesus Christ his Son cleanseth us from all sin. (1 Jn. 1:6-7)

Obviously, then, the association of darkness with sin is an immediate corollary of the truth that God is light. Solomon spoke of evil men "who leave the paths of uprightness, to walk in the ways of darkness" (Pr. 2:13). Likewise, "the way of the wicked is as darkness: they know not at what they stumble" (Pr. 4:19).

John's gospel includes what is perhaps the most famous verse in the Bible: "For God so loved the world, that he gave his only begotten Son, that whosoever believeth in him should not perish, but have everlasting life" (Jn. 3:16). What about those who don't believe? John says they are condemned for their unbelief (v. 18). It isn't mere intellectual objections that exclude them from eternal life, however. Rather,

> this is the condemnation, that light is come into the world, and men loved darkness rather than light, because their deeds were evil. For every one that doeth evil hateth the light, neither cometh to the light, lest his deeds should be reproved. But he that doeth truth cometh to the light, that his deeds may be made manifest, that they are wrought in God. (Jn. 3:19-21)

The Darkness of Judgment

Of necessity, sin requires judgment. Darkness, therefore, is not only an fitting metaphor for sin, but a literal form of punishment for it as well. The eighth plague on Egypt is an excellent example:

> And the LORD said unto Moses, Stretch out thine hand toward heaven, that there may be darkness over the land of Egypt, even dark-

> ness which may be felt. And Moses stretched
> forth his hand toward heaven; and there was
> a thick darkness in all the land of Egypt three
> days: they saw not one another, neither rose
> any from his place for three days: but all the
> children of Israel had light in their dwellings.
> (Ex. 10:21-23)

The darkness here was qualified as "darkness
which may be felt" and "thick darkness." And it
was as limited as it was intense, for the children
of Israel in the neighboring land of Goshen had
light, while the nearby Egyptians had none.

Deliverance From Darkness

However, even when darkness is a form of
judgment, God's great mercy provides deliverance
and redemption from it. Psalm 107 speaks of several situations where people were delivered by the
mercy of God, including those who

> sat in darkness and the deepest gloom, pris-
> oners suffering in iron chains, for they had
> rebelled against the words of God and de-
> spised the counsel of the Most High. So he
> subjected them to bitter labor; they stumbled,
> and there was no one to help. Then they cried
> to the LORD in their trouble, and he saved
> them from their distress. He brought them out
> of darkness and the deepest gloom and broke
> away their chains. (Ps. 107:10-14, NIV)

Of course, Christ, who spoke of Himself

as "the light of the world" (Jn. 8:12), is the greatest expression of God's willingness to forgive sinners and deliver them from darkness. Predicting
the first coming of Christ, Isaiah writes, "the
people that walked in darkness have seen a great
light: they that dwell in the land of the shadow of
death, upon them hath the light shined" (Isa. 9:2).
Naturally, the second coming of Christ will have
a similar impact:

> Arise, shine; for thy light is come, and the
> glory of the LORD is risen upon thee. For, be-
> hold, the darkness shall cover the earth, and
> gross darkness the people: but the LORD shall
> arise upon thee, and his glory shall be seen
> upon thee. And the Gentiles shall come to
> thy light, and kings to the brightness of thy
> rising. (Isa. 60:1-3)

In the most extreme display of God's pas-
sion for sinners and His wrath and judgment for
sin, the light of the world was crucified. For three
hours that afternoon, darkness blanketed the land
while the Son of God hung upon the cross (Mt.
27:45; Mk. 15:33; Lk. 23:44). Yet in that one act
of love and judgment combined, true deliverance
was provided from darkness, for all who will re-
pent and believe. To make His deliverance known
to all men, Jesus sent Paul to the Gentiles, "to
open their eyes, and to turn them from darkness
to light, and from the power of Satan unto God,
that they may receive forgiveness of sins, and in-

heritance among them which are sanctified by faith that is in me" (Acts 26:18).

The Former Darkness

The New Testament often uses the themes of darkness and light to contrast our former life with newness of life in Christ. Paul reminded the Ephesians, "for ye were sometimes darkness, but now are ye light in the Lord: walk as children of light" (Eph. 5:8). As a result of their new identity, they were to "have no fellowship with the unfruitful works of darkness" (Eph. 5:11). Paul exhorted the Colossians to join him in

> giving thanks unto the Father, which hath made us meet to be partakers of the inheritance of the saints in light: who hath delivered us from the power of darkness, and hath translated us into the kingdom of his dear Son: in whom we have redemption through his blood, even the forgiveness of sins. (Col. 1:12-14)

Likewise, Peter reminded his readers,

> But ye are a chosen generation, a royal priesthood, an holy nation, a peculiar people; that ye should shew forth the praises of him who hath called you out of darkness into his marvellous light. (1 Pet. 2:9)

However, such a calling does not come without responsibilities to walk it out in daily living. Therefore, Paul wrote to the Romans:

> The night is far spent, the day is at hand: let
> us therefore cast off the works of darkness, and
> let us put on the armour of light. Let us walk
> honestly, as in the day; not in rioting and
> drunkenness, not in chambering and wanton-
> ness, not in strife and envying. But put ye on
> the Lord Jesus Christ, and make not provi-
> sion for the flesh, to fulfil the lusts thereof.
> (Rom. 13:12-14)

Rejecting the Light

But there are many who have resisted all appeals to come out of darkness and into light, for they prefer the darkness to the light (Jn. 3:19). Jesus urged His hearers, "Yet a little while is the light with you. Walk while ye have the light, lest darkness come upon you: for he that walketh in darkness knoweth not whither he goeth" (Jn. 12:35). Centuries earlier, Jeremiah appealed to backslidden Israel,

> Give glory to the LORD your God, before he
> cause darkness, and before your feet stumble
> upon the dark mountains, and, while ye look
> for light, he turn it into the shadow of death,
> and make it gross darkness. (Jer. 13:16)

Knowing many would refuse to heed such calls, Jesus often spoke of those who would be excluded from the kingdom, saying they would be "cast into outer darkness: there shall be weeping and gnash-ing of teeth" (Mt. 8:12; 22:13; 25:30). Warning of certain judgment for false teachers and their followers, Peter reminded his readers that "God spared not the angels that sinned, but cast them down to hell, and delivered them into chains of darkness, to be reserved unto judgment" (2 Pet. 2:4; Jude 6). But for those who persist in sin, "the mist of darkness is reserved for ever" (2 Pet. 2:17; Jude 13). And when Elymas the sorcerer opposed the ministry of Paul and Barnabas, he received an immediate token of the darkness to come:

> Paul, filled with the Holy Spirit, looked straight at Elymas and said, "You are a child of the devil and an enemy of everything that is right! You are full of all kinds of deceit and trickery. Will you never stop perverting the right ways of the Lord? Now the hand of the Lord is against you. You are going to be blind, and for a time you will be unable to see the light of the sun." Immediately mist and darkness came over him, and he groped about, seeking someone to lead him by the hand. (Acts 13:9-11, NIV)

The Powers of Darkness

In the most blatant rejection of light that anyone has ever displayed, Lucifer, the "son of the morning" (Isa. 14:12), whose name meant "light-bearer," became the prince of darkness himself. With perverse mockery of his former position as "the anointed cherub" (Ezek. 28:14), Paul tells us that "Satan himself is transformed into an angel of light" (2 Cor. 11:14). Always one to seize any advantage he can, Satan and his minions work diligently to prevent those in darkness from coming to the light:

> But if our gospel be hid, it is hid to them that are lost: in whom the god of this world hath blinded the minds of them which believe not, lest the light of the glorious gospel of Christ, who is the image of God, should shine unto them. (2 Cor. 4:3-4)

Thus, believers must engage in spiritual warfare:

> for we wrestle not against flesh and blood, but against principalities, against powers, against the rulers of the darkness of this world, against spiritual wickedness in high places. (Eph. 6:12)

A Day of Darkness

As the curtains prepare to fall on the earth's second sinful career, darkness accompanies the event. As the prophet Joel predicts, "The sun shall be turned into darkness, and the moon into blood, before the great and terrible day of the LORD come" (Joel 2:31). Zephaniah says, "that day is a day of wrath, a day of trouble and distress, a day of wasteness and desolation, a day of darkness and gloominess, a day of clouds and thick darkness" (Zeph. 1:15).

Back to Genesis

Believe it or not, the examples above fall far short of exhausting what Scripture actually teaches about darkness. From these passages we've discovered that darkness portrays all life apart from God, who is light. Sin in particular is represented by darkness, which thus makes darkness a logical form of judgment for sin. In many instances of judgment, it is more than just a metaphor; literal darkness is involved.

Darkness, therefore, is much more than the mere absence of light; it is the very antithesis of light. It stands in malevolent opposition to all that light represents. In fact, when darkness is mentioned in Scripture, it rarely refers to ordinary nighttime. On the contrary, it nearly always signifies something bad, something wrong, something evil.

We've already learned that the condition of the earth in the first part of Genesis 1:2 could not possibly describe the initial stages of original creation. And we've seen that before he fell, Lucifer ruled entire nations on earth in a time before Adam. Furthermore, Lucifer's rebellion resulted in the earth's first sinful career. In order to produce the second sinless state into which God introduced Adam and Eve, God first had to annihilate the pre-Adamite world. The resulting destruction matches the description of the original Hebrew for "without form, and void."

Now, add to all this what we now know about the Bible's general assessment of darkness, and re-read Genesis 1:2. "And the earth was without form, and void; and darkness was upon the face of the deep." The conjunction "and" clearly joins this darkness to the chaos of the preceding phrase. It is, therefore, a darkness of judgment rather than a darkness of early creation.

Finally, don't forget that "God is light, and in him is no darkness at all" (1 Jn. 1:5). This one statement is enough to upset the entire traditional view of creation, if you stop and think about it. In the traditional interpretation of Genesis 1:2, the darkness is simply the natural state of things prior to the initial creation of light. But God *is* light! He didn't *become* light in Genesis 1:3; He has always been light, and always will be. In fact, Revelation 22:5 tells us of a time when not only will there be no night, but not even the light of the sun will be needed, for God Himself shall be the light. Therefore, the darkness in Genesis 1:2 does not describe some vague nothingness before creation. Rather, it was intentional. And, consistent with the rest of Scripture, it was a form of judgment.

LUCIFER'S FLOOD

Though we've examined Genesis 1:2 many times now, we haven't exhausted it. Yet another piece of the puzzle remains: "And the earth was without form, and void; and darkness was upon the face of the deep. And the Spirit of God moved upon the face of the waters." Have you noticed the fact that the earth in this verse is under water? So far, we've seen that each description in this verse perfectly conforms to the idea of the destruction of the pre-Adamite world. These waters covering the earth are no different. In the context of judgment, such waters could only indicate a global deluge, which we call Lucifer's flood.

Flood waters covered the earth in Noah's day as God judged fallen humanity and started over with Noah and his family. So there is a solid biblical precedent for interpreting a global flood as a form of judgment. And, as everything else in Genesis 1:2 points to a judgment greater than that in Noah's day, Lucifer's flood should follow suit. Not only does the immediate context support this claim, but other passages of Scripture will also testify to two great floods on earth, the lesser of which was Noah's.

We'll find in Psalms, and again in 2 Peter, that the writers mention a flood more destructive than the judgment unleashed on the people of Noah's day. We'll take a further look at these verses as we examine some of the key differences between these two catastrophic events.

If history does indeed bear record of two floods of worldwide proportions, we would expect to find a similarity in the individual accounts, as well as an overlapping of the sequence of events due to the correspondence between the two cataclysms. Therefore, it should come as no surprise that the records of the earth's two floods could mistakenly be understood as referring to a single event. And indeed, we find this is often the case.

On the other hand, a closer examination of the biblical record will reveal extensive dissimilarities between the two catastrophes.

Insights From Psalm 104

Psalm 104 is a beautiful psalm of praise to God for His creation and providence. However, like the Genesis material, hints of the pre-Adamite world are easily overlooked. We are particularly reminded of the first verses of Genesis when the psalmist praises God for being the one

> Who laid the foundations of the earth, that it should not be removed for ever. Thou coveredst it with the deep as with a garment: the waters stood above the mountains. (Ps. 104:5-6)

In the traditional view, the early stages of creation have the earth covered with water. The same imagery appears here in Psalm 104. However, as we've already seen, the details of Genesis 1:2 vividly describe the aftermath of the destruction of the pre-Adamite world, rather than God's initial handiwork on a pristine earth. Again, the same is true of the floodwaters in Psalm 104. The only other time we know of where water covered the mountains was Noah's flood. When that flood was over, the waters slowly and naturally abated. But here the psalmist declares that "at thy rebuke they fled; at the voice of thy thunder they hasted away" (Ps. 104:7). In addition, we read in the ninth verse that "Thou hast set a bound that they may not pass over; that they turn not again to cover the earth." This also parallels the Genesis account:

> And God said, Let the waters under the heaven be gathered together unto one place, and let the dry land appear: and it was so. And God called the dry land Earth; and the gathering together of the waters called he Seas: and God saw that it was good. (Gen. 1:9-10)

Thus in Psalm 104:5-9 we have another description of the destruction of the world before Adam and of the restoration of the earth out of that flood. First the flood is described as having come upon the earth after the foundations of the earth were laid, and the waters are seen to be standing above the mountains. Then the passage concludes by explaining how the flood was removed from the earth so that it could be inhabited again.

Peter's Teaching on Lucifer's Flood

In his second epistle Peter makes the following statement:

> Knowing this first, that there shall come in the last days scoffers, walking after their own lusts, and saying, where is the promise of his coming? For since the fathers fell asleep, all things continue as they were from the beginning of the creation. For this they willingly are ignorant of, that by the word of God the

heavens were of old, and the earth standing
out of the water and in the water. Whereby
the world that then was, being overflowed
with water, perished: but the heavens and the
earth, which are now, by the same word are
kept in store, reserved unto fire against the
day of judgment and perdition of ungodly
men. (2 Pet. 3:3-7)

The earth "standing out of the water and in the
water" is a reference to a flood. But it can't be
Noah's flood, for in verse five Peter claims that
scoffers are ignorant of the flood of which he
speaks. The Greek word for "ignorant" in 2 Peter
3:5 is *lanthano*, translated elsewhere "hid" and
"hidden" (Mk. 7:24; Lk. 8:47; Acts 26:26) and
"unawares" (Heb. 13:2). Peter is saying that the
truth of the flood that destroyed the original social system was obscured. What was it that was
hidden from the scoffers, or of what were they
unaware? It must have been the destruction of a
world before Adam, not the flood of Noah's day.
The scoffers of whom Peter was speaking were
obviously aware of Noah's flood, but the facts concerning the deluge that destroyed the pre-Adamite
world were hidden from them, as it is for many in
our day.

Many difficult questions relating to the
flood account are resolved when we plug a pre-
Adamite world into the equation. On the other
hand, if we embrace the position that the flood
which destroyed "the world that then was" is the

same flood that partly destroyed the social system in Noah's day, we find ourselves with a lot of questions without answers. Let's look at where the trail will lead if we choose to ignore the possibility of a pre-Adamite world.

Different Social Systems?

Peter says that "the world [*kosmos*, social system[1]] that then was" perished because of a flood. The Greek word for "perish" is *apollumi* which means to perish or destroy. We find this word used often in the New Testament, and it means exactly what it says.

Of course, the first thing that comes to mind is the flood of Noah's day which resulted in the mass destruction of all life on earth, apart from that which was preserved in the ark. The Genesis account offers this vivid description:

> And all flesh died that moved upon the earth, both of fowl, and of cattle, and of beast, and of every creeping thing that creepeth upon the earth, and every man: all in whose nostrils was the breath of life, of all that was in the dry land, died. And every living substance was destroyed which was upon the face of the ground, both man, and cattle, and the creeping things, and the fowl of the heaven; and they were destroyed from the earth: and Noah only remained alive, and they that were with

---

1. The word *kosmos* means "social system" rather than "world" in the planetary sense. This is explained in greater detail in the next chapter.

him in the ark. And the waters prevailed upon
the earth an hundred and fifty days. (Gen.
7:21-24)

So far, so good. We have a flood, and we
have the extermination of virtually all life on earth.
But there are two main problems. First, Adam's
line was preserved through Noah, thus ensuring
the continuation of the social order set in place
generations earlier. Second, and more important,
the survival of Noah and his family ensured the
future accomplishment of the covenant God
made with Adam and Eve. When cursing the serpent, God said, "And I will put enmity between
thee and the woman, and between thy seed and
her seed; it shall bruise thy head, and thou shalt
bruise his heel (Gen. 3:15)." If Adam's lineage
had been completely destroyed during Noah's day,
this covenant would never have come to pass. God
had made a promise that through Adam and Eve
a savior would come, and indeed He did. Jesus
Christ was a descendant of Adam, through Noah,
and was the fulfillment of the promise made 6,000
years ago.

Different Floods?
If there were no pre-Adamite world and
no flood sent in judgment of Lucifer's sin, then
we would expect that references made by the
apostle Peter to a worldwide flood would point to
the Genesis account of Noah and his family. But

always, without exception, Peter makes it very clear when he refers to the flood of Noah. In 1 Peter 3:20 he says that "God waited in the days of Noah, while the ark was a preparing, wherein few, that is, eight souls were saved by water." And 2 Peter 2:5 states that God "spared not the old world, but saved Noah the eighth person, a preacher of righteousness, bringing in the flood upon the world of the ungodly."

On the other hand, when Peter states that the entire social system "that then was" perished by water, we have to conclude that he is not speaking of the flood of Noah's day, for there is no reference to Noah or any survivors. And surely the scoffers referred to by Peter in verse three would not be so ignorant as to believe that the entire social system perished in Noah's flood, or they themselves would not be present to scoff!

Different Creation?

We've already looked at Peter's statement that the "world that then was, being overflowed with water, perished." We've suggested that the world Peter refers to is a pre-Adamite creation. But we've set that aside for the time being to pursue another path, and already we have encountered some obstacles along the way. Let's press on, though, and see what happens if we assume the "world that then was" is a reference to the earth as it existed prior to Noah's flood.

Peter states that the world (*kosmos*, social

order) "that then was" was flooded and perished. He contrasts that world with the earth on which we now live in verse seven, and argues that the earth is now reserved for judgment. Up to this point, we can fit most of Peter's references within the context of Noah's flood. If we ignore the fact that the social order of Noah's day didn't perish during the flood of Genesis 8, and if we ignore the fact that Peter claims that scoffers are ignorant of the flood of which he speaks, we may be able to fit this piece of text into our puzzle. But there's another catch in verse seven where Peter speaks of the "heavens and the earth, which are now." Of course, the heavens of which he speaks are the atmospheric heavens and not the realm inhabited by God. If there are heavens "which are now," then by implication the heavens have undergone the same sort of transformation as the earth. Following this line of reasoning, the present heavens and the earth would have to have been created in Noah's day in order to make "the heavens and the earth which are now." But during Noah's flood there was no re-creation of the heavens; they underwent no change at all.

Since Peter implies a past change in the structure of the heavens, it must have occurred at some point in the past. Because we have no indication in Scripture of a change in the heavens from Adam's day till the present, any alteration must have taken place before the six days of Genesis 1. Therefore, only a pre-Adamite creation can explain the facts as recorded by Peter.

Jeremiah's Vision of Chaos

God revealed to the prophet Jeremiah a vision of desolation on the earth in order to warn Israel of His impending judgment on the land for their rebellion:

> I beheld the earth, and, lo, it was without form, and void; and the heavens, and they had no light. I beheld the mountains, and, lo, they trembled, and all the hills moved lightly. I beheld, and, lo, there was no man, and all the birds of the heavens were fled. I beheld, and, lo, the fruitful place was a wilderness, and all the cities thereof were broken down at the presence of the Lord, and by his fierce anger. For thus hath the Lord said, The whole land shall be desolate; yet I will not make a full end. (Jer. 4:23-27)

Jeremiah is describing events in this passage that took place sometime in the historical framework of God's dealings with man. There is a contrast made in these verses between the whole earth being totally desolate and the land of Israel being partially desolate. The purpose of this juxtaposition was to show how utterly God had cursed the earth at one time because of sin, so the Israelites could have a picture of the extent of the destruction which would result from their continued rebellion. However, God promised the Israelites that He would "not make a full end" of the earth, as

He had done in the earlier judgment described by the prophet.

According to Jeremiah's vision, there had at one time been men on the earth, but not one was left following the incredible judgment poured out by God. Although there had been cities inhabited by men and fruitful places covering the earth, not one remained. The cities were broken down, and every man and animal was totally destroyed by the presence of the Lord and by His fierce anger.

Apparently there was a social system on the earth prior to this devastation. Like the cities and the fruitful places, this social order was completely destroyed. If Jeremiah saw the total destruction of life on earth, then there must have been such a judgment, clearly brought about by God's wrath. The Bible declares that God is "slow to anger, and plenteous in mercy . . . neither will he keep his anger forever" (Ps. 103:8-9). Therefore the causes of God's anger must have been many and long in duration and must have continued until no mercy could be shown.

Once again, we find a passage that makes reference to a global cataclysm, and we're faced with the task of pinpointing the specific event the author had in mind. So far we've learned that Jeremiah sees cities, but they've been destroyed. The earth lies desolate because of the terrible judgment of God. Earthquakes shake the mountains, and the fruitful places have become barren and lifeless. Although there is no mention of a flood, the only time such incredible devastation could have occurred was either during Noah's flood, or during the time period between the first two verses of Genesis. We believe the evidence argues clearly for the latter.

First, Jeremiah sees the earth "without form, and void." The only other place in the entire Old Testament where this Hebrew phrase is used is Genesis 1:2. It stands to reason, then, that the empty desolation described by the Hebrew words *tohuw* and *bohuw* is the same in both passages. Furthermore, to complete the parallel, Jeremiah also envisioned the darkness of the heavens.[2] In spite of how destructive Noah's flood was, it just doesn't match the devastation described in our previous study of Genesis 1:2. (See the detailed contrast of Lucifer's and Noah's floods, below.)

---

2. Incidentally, light could have been withheld from the earth for decades, centuries or more. It's at least possible that this could have extended the polar ice fields deep into equatorial regions. Furthermore, the earthquake described by Jeremiah could have had a direct impact on the deposition of the plant and animal remains of the pre-Adamite world. Flora and fauna could have been relocated in strata deeper than those in which they were originally deposited. All this may partially explain the apparent antiquity of the archaeological record. It is also interesting to note Ferrar Fenton's translation (*The Complete Bible in Modern English*, S. W. Partridge & Co., London, 1906) of Genesis 1:2 which reads, "But the Earth was unorganized and empty; and darkness covered its *convulsed surface*; while the breath of God rocked the surface of its waters" (italics added). Thus, Fenton seems to concur that the earth went through a period of convulsions which could be consistent with earthquakes. If so, this strengthens even more the parallel between Jeremiah's vision and Genesis 1:2.

Second, the language of Jeremiah 4:23-27 cannot be understood figuratively, for it is clearly a literal description of a literal judgment on a literal earth and on real cities, mountains, hills, fruitful places, men, birds, and animals. There is no indication that this passage is metaphorical and there is no necessity to make it so. The impending judgment on the land of Israel was very real; so the contrasting judgment on the whole earth, which illustrates how the land of Israel was to be judged, must also be a literal judgment.

Besides the textual difficulty in treating the Jeremiah passage in a metaphorical sense, there are other problems as well. One of the greatest difficulties involves defining boundaries when forcing a figurative interpretation on a passage that does not explicitly call for a non-literal reading. In other words, if we can interpret the facts presented in Jeremiah 4 figuratively, then on the same grounds we can interpret figuratively the facts of creation recorded in the Genesis account. On this basis of personal opinion we can assign a figurative interpretation to any portion of Scripture. But in doing so we would undermine the foundation of the Bible itself; we would be left without any solid ground on which to build an accurate understanding of any scriptural text.

If a passage is to be interpreted figuratively when there is a possibility for a literal interpretation, then we must have definite scriptural authority to do so. Using God's Word as our authority, we lessen the possibility of "dividing the word of truth" based on the opinion of man. If we will give a literal interpretation to what can be interpreted literally, we'll have a commonsense method of understanding God's Word and a solid base for the application of Scripture to our daily lives. Such an approach to the study of the Bible can guide us in our understanding of difficult passages. Even the study of secular literature can lend some insight into this area. When we grab a book off a library shelf and open its pages, we naturally assume as we read the text that repeated descriptions of an event are references to the same event, unless the author indicates otherwise. Since we use familiar logic with secular books, why do we hesitate to apply the same approach to the study of God's Word? Because we have read exactly the same words in Genesis 1:2 as we read in Jeremiah 4:23, we naturally conclude that they refer to the same event.

Contrasting the Flood Accounts

The flood of Noah's day was an act of judgment passed upon men because of sin. Those of us who understand the Genesis 8 account as a literal event do not doubt the extent of the destruction described by Moses. Scripture is clear that except for Moses and his family, all men and animals were destroyed as a result of God's judgment. There are those who claim the flood narrative is a fable, but no one doubts the existence of men prior to Noah's flood. Why then doubt the existence of a pre-Adamite world which was destroyed by the flood of Genesis 1:2? That this was a greater flood than the one of Noah's time, and an act of greater judgment in punishment of more horrible sins is clear from the following contrasts:

Lucifer's	Noah's
1 Earth made waste (Gen. 1:2; Jer. 4:23)	Not made waste (Gen. 8:11-12, 22)
2 Earth made empty (Gen. 1:2; Jer. 4:23)	Not made empty (Gen. 6:17-22; 8:16)
3 Earth made totally dark (Gen. 1:2; Jer. 4:23)	Not made totally dark (Gen. 8:6-22)
4 No light from heaven (Gen. 1:2; Jer. 4:23)	Light from heaven (Gen. 8:6-22)
5 No days (Gen. 1:2-5)	Days (Gen. 8:1-22)
6 All vegetation destroyed (Jer. 4:23-26)	Vegetation left (Gen. 8:11-12, 22)
7 No continual abating of waters off the earth (Gen. 1:6-12)	Continual abating of waters off earth (Gen. 8:1-14)
8 Waters taken off earth in one day (Gen. 1:10)	Months abating off earth (Gen. 8:1-14)
9 Supernatural work of taking waters off earth (Gen. 1:6-12)	Natural work of taking waters off the earth (Gen. 8:1-14)
10 God rebuked the waters (Gen. 1:6-12; Ps. 104:7)	No rebuke of the waters (Gen. 8:1-14)
11 Waters hasted away (Ps. 104:7)	Waters gradually receded (Gen. 8:1-14)
12 God set bounds for waters (Ps. 104:9)	Bounds already set (Gen. 1:6-12; 8:2)
13 All fish destroyed because sun withheld from earth (1:2, 20-23; Jer. 4:23-26)	No fish destroyed, only the land animals (Gen. 6:18 - 8:22)

14	No fowls left (Gen. 1:20; Jer. 4:25)	Fowls preserved (Gen. 6:20; 8:17)
15	No animals left (Gen. 1:24-25; 2:19)	Animals preserved (Gen. 6:20; 8:17)
16	No man left (Gen. 1:26-28; Jer. 4:25)	Eight men and women saved (Gen. 6:18)
17	No social system left (2 Pet. 3:6; Jer. 4:23-26)	A social system left (Gen. 6:18; 8:22; 2 Pet. 2:5)
18	No ark made to save life (Jer. 4:23-26; 2 Pet. 3:6-7)	An ark made to save life (Gen. 6:14-22; 1 Pet. 3:20)
19	Cause: fall of Satan (Isa. 14:12-14; Jer. 4:23-26; Ezek. 28: 11-17)	Cause: wickedness of man and fallen angels (Gen. 6:1-13)
20	Result: necessary to make new fish, fowl, animals, man, vegetation (Gen. 1:3 - 2:25)	Result: no new creations were made, for all things were preserved (Gen. 6:18 - 8:22)

The flood of Noah's day lasted over a year, yet vegetation was not destroyed. But as a result of the flood sent in judgment upon Lucifer, the fruitful places became a wilderness (Jer. 4:23-26). New vegetation had to be planted during the six days of re-creation, for the earth was totally desolate (Gen. 1:11-12; 2:5, 8-17). This indicates that Lucifer's flood was of a much longer duration than Noah's and, without doubt, was a judgment for a more serious rebellion—a complete rebellion of the pre-Adamite world.

Results of the Flood

Evidence for a great catastrophe that resulted in the destruction of the pre-Adamite world can be found in Scripture, as we have seen, but we can look to the sciences as well for further

verification. Most scientists assert that the earth
went through at least one great catastrophe at an
unknown period in the past. Many animal remains have been discovered that indicate a sud-
den environmental calamity befalling large popu-
lations. Speaking of the flood of Noah, but more
accurately describing the results of the flood
which destroyed the pre-Adamite world, Douglas
B. Sharp states that the flood explains the geologic column, which is the order of the strata and
the fossils found in them:

> Hydrodynamic sorting action of the water,
> habitats, the ability of an animal to escape
> the flood and ecological zones are all factors
> which would have produced fossil layers. This
> explanation handles the problem of out-of-
> order strata and fossils, which is a nasty prob-
> lem for evolutionists. . . . In many places, large
> fossils such as trees extend through several
> strata. Rapid burial is also necessary for coal
> and oil formation and for fossilization, other-
> wise the normal process of decay would com-
> pletely disintegrate the organisms, even the
> bones.[3]

We've mentioned briefly that many fossils
have been found which were evidently the result
of a great catastrophe, being entombed in the
strata instead of being slowly buried by sedimen-
tation over millions of years. During Lucifer's

---

3. Douglas B. Sharp, *Creation Models*. <http://www.sojourn.com/
~revev/web/models.html>. 3 Nov 1996.

flood God turned the earth upside down by earthquakes. In Peleg's time, we read of a great division of the earth. It is interesting that while we have only a brief mention of this catastrophic event, it was significant enough to define an entire generation in the genealogical record: "And unto Eber were born two sons: the name of one was Peleg; for in his days was the earth divided; and his brother's name was Joktan" (Gen. 10:25).

It's at least possible that this short account of a division of the earth is a reference to a shifting of the continents and a great division of land masses. Lucifer's flood and the division of the earth in Peleg's day may well account for much of the fossil record and help to explain many questions which otherwise remain unanswered by other creationist theories.

As we've seen, the other creationist theories struggle to account for scientific evidence which points to an old earth. Part of the difficulty is that these theories are attempting to force the scientific data into a mold that is simply not large enough to contain it. Most creationist theories cannot account for an old earth because they have not factored into the equation the existence of the pre-Adamite world. Only an understanding of an original creation of the earth that preceded the destruction of Genesis 1:2 can shed light on the questions posed by the scientific evidence. The existence and overthrow of the pre-Adamite world resolves the following questions:

Why are we finding remains of animals that never existed in Adam's day? Quite simply, these animals were a part of the original creation of the earth and were destroyed and buried with the destruction of the earth following Lucifer's rebellion. The Bible doesn't tell us how long Lucifer was allowed to remain in rebellion against God before he was cast back down to the earth in judgment. The earth could have existed in a sinful state as a result of Lucifer's sin, with animals living and dying for centuries before God judged Lucifer and his rebellious followers.

How did the remains of animals get thousands of feet in the earth underneath many layers of solid rock if there was no catastrophe as described in Gen. 1:2; Jer. 4:23-26; and 2 Pet. 3:5-6? The division of the earth in Peleg's day could account for a part of the fossil record. Noah's flood, however, could not have resulted in the extensive deposits found deep beneath the earth on a worldwide scale, and no other global cataclysm has happened since Adam.

Why do we find geological evidence pointing to an earth that is much older than Adam's creation about 6,000 years ago? This is easily explained when we understand that the earth was created in the dateless past, underwent cataclysmic changes during the judgment brought about by Lucifer's rebellion, and was re-created about 6,000 years ago.

Chapter 6 _____

THE WORLD THAT
THEN WAS

When we first began to challenge the traditional view of the creation account, we spent most of our time examining in great detail the implications of Genesis 1:2. What we found clearly indicated that there was a significant gap between the first two verses in the Bible. The second verse couldn't possibly fit in the scheme of original creation, for it bore all the marks of a cataclysmic judgment. Further research into the fall of Lucifer helped us fill in the gap with details of the existence and overthrow of the pre-Adamite world. The emblems of judgment that emerged in every facet of Genesis 1:2 now had a chronological context that fit the picture we were seeing.

In spite of all this, there is a sense in which

you could say that our work thus far has essentially been reading between the lines. No text to this point has explicitly spelled out the doctrine of the pre-Adamite world. Clues have been uncovered certainly, and compelling clues at that — clues which have enabled us to piece the concept together like an intriguing puzzle. In this chapter, however, we will explore a text that comes very close to being an actual exposition of this teaching.

A Social System Before Adam

We belong to a social order which began with the creation of Adam and Eve and which will continue throughout eternity. Extending in an unbroken chain from Adam's day till ours, the continuity of this social system was almost broken during the flood of Noah's day. But God saved Noah and his family, and thus assured the perpetuation of Adam's line. But there was another social order, one which must have existed before God fashioned Adam from the dust of the earth. Peter discusses this social order in his second epistle. He begins the third chapter by stirring his readers to remembrance:

> Knowing this first, that there shall come in the last days scoffers, walking after their own lusts, and saying, Where is the promise of his coming? for since the fathers fell asleep, all things continue as they were from the beginning of the creation. For this they willingly

> are ignorant of, that by the word of God the
> heavens were of old, and the earth standing
> out of the water and in the water: whereby
> the world that then was, being overflowed
> with water, perished: but the heavens and the
> earth, which are now, by the same word are
> kept in store, reserved unto fire against the
> day of judgment and perdition of ungodly
> men. (2 Pet. 3:3-7)

In this passage we have strong scriptural
evidence that two social systems have existed at
separate times in the earth's history. Support for
this view comes from the statements which make
reference to "the world that then was" and "the
heavens and the earth, which are now." Evidently,
a social order existed prior to the creation of the
one in which we now live.

The Significance of Kosmos
When Peter alludes to "the world that then
was," he uses the Greek word *kosmos* which occurs 187 times in the New Testament, translated
"world" every time but once. In the immediate
context of "the heavens . . . and the earth standing out of the water and in the water" it would
appear at first that *kosmos* refers to the world in a
physical sense, equivalent to "planet." This, however, is not the case.

To be sure, there are a few places where
kosmos is used in a physical (hence, *cosmic*) sense.
John, for example, stated that if everything Jesus

did had been recorded, "even the world itself could not contain the books that should be written" (Jn. 21:25). In his famous sermon on Mars' hill, Paul proclaimed that "God that made the world and all things therein, seeing that he is Lord of heaven and earth, dwelleth not in temples made with hands" (Acts 17:24). Finally, declaring the validity of natural revelation, Paul told the Romans that

> the invisible things of him from the creation of the world are clearly seen, being understood by the things that are made, even his eternal power and Godhead; so that they are without excuse. (Rom. 1:20)

For the most part, however, the word *kosmos* refers to the world full of *people*, organized by governments and social systems. A sample of the many passages where *kosmos* is used will demonstrate this truth. In the midst of his wilderness temptations the devil showed Jesus "all the kingdoms of the world, and the glory of them" (Mt. 4:8). He was offering Jesus rulership of the world's population, not ownership of a rock in space. In the Sermon on the Mount Jesus told His followers, "Ye are the light of the world" (Mt. 5:14). The sun is the light to the earth, but believers are the light to the lost souls who populate the planet. Directing attention to Jesus, John the Baptist said, "Behold, the Lamb of God, which taketh away the sin of the world" (Jn. 1:29). And finally, in a text which most of us learned as children, we read:

> For God so loved the world, that he gave his
> only begotten Son, that whosoever believeth
> in him should not perish, but have everlast-
> ing life. For God sent not his Son into the world
> to condemn the world; but that the world
> through him might be saved. (Jn. 3:16-17)

Obviously, redemption of the planet isn't the issue here, but the salvation of humanity.

So, when Peter speaks of "the world that
then was," he is contrasting a pre-existing social
order with the one of which we are a part. He
further reinforces the idea of a world destroyed
and made new again with his reference to "the
heavens and the earth, which are now."

A Rational Interpretation
To prove that "the world that then was"
refers to the pre-Adamite world, consider first that
this is the most literal interpretation of the passage. Peter clearly expresses the idea of a world
destroyed and given life again in these two verses.
Let's take another look at Peter's statement, this
time with added emphasis:

> By the word of God the heavens *were of old*,
> and the earth standing out of the water and
> in the water. Whereby the world [social or-
> der] *that then was* [i.e., of old, and *before* the
> heavens and the earth *which are now*], being
> overflowed with water perished: but the heav-

ens and the earth, *which are now* [*after* the
world *that then was*], by the same word are
kept in store, reserved unto fire against the day
of judgment and perdition of ungodly men.

Second, if "the world that then was" is the
same as that which existed between Adam and
the flood of Noah, then God made "the heavens
and the earth which are now" *since* the flood of
Noah. Although this is a popular interpretation
of the passage, it is not taught anywhere in Scripture. There is no statement in either the Old or
New Testaments that indicates that the heavens
and the earth "which are now" differ from what
they were between the time of Adam and Noah.
On the contrary, we have a clear record that in
six days God made "the heavens and the earth,
which are now," and there is no reference to a
new creation following the flood of Noah.

Is it possible that Noah's flood could have
resulted in a permanent change in the heavens
and the earth? Thumb through the pages of Scripture and you'll find no indication of a restructur-
ing of the heavens in any way. Neither does Scripture record a re-creation of the earth during this
time. There was no change in the earth's social
system after Noah's flood, for the society that followed was merely an extension through Noah's
family of the system which started with Adam.
Likewise, the earth, seas, and plant and animal
life remained the same after the flood as before.

Three Separate Social Systems

Peter makes it clear that there are three very distinct and separate periods in the annals of the earth's history. The first period has passed and we currently live in the second. But a third sinless state will exist in the future, and in the following verses the apostle lets us look through his eyes to a future day when righteousness will dwell in the earth:

> But the day of the Lord will come as a thief in the night; in the which the heavens shall pass away with a great noise, and the elements shall melt with fervent heat, the earth also and the works that are therein shall be burned up. Seeing then that all these things shall be dissolved, what manner of persons ought ye to be in all holy conversation and godliness, Looking for and hasting unto the coming of the day of God, wherein the heavens being on fire shall be dissolved, and the elements shall melt with fervent heat? Nevertheless we, according to his promise, look for new heavens and a new earth, wherein dwelleth righteousness. (2 Pet. 3:10-13)

Before our eyes Peter spreads wide the panorama of history, beginning with the social system "that then was." Peter explains that the social order of which we are now a part is also doomed for judgment, as was the society which existed before Adam's creation. God's righteousness is equaled only by His mercy, but the day will come

in which the earth will once again face the judgment of God. This final judgment will precede
the final restoration of the earth, referred to by
Peter as the "new heavens and a new earth" that
are to come (vv. 5-7, 13). The new heavens and
new earth "wherein dwelleth righteousness" will
exist after the current age.

Thus we see three social systems established during the three phases of the earth's existence: first, the original social system which existed before Adam; second, the current system
which began with Adam's creation and which will
continue through the renovation of the new heavens and new earth; and third, the new heavens
and earth "wherein dwelleth righteousness."[1]

Two distinct social systems have existed on
the earth and both have failed to follow God's
moral law, according to Peter. God must have
decreed judgment for "the world that then was,"
or it would not have been destroyed to make room
for the present social system. There will be an
end to the earth's present sinful condition, for the
current heavens and earth "are kept in store, reserved unto fire against the day of judgment and
perdition of ungodly men" (2 Pet. 3:7). The de-

---

1. Dake's understanding of this third social system does not entail a
complete destruction of humanity as in the overthrow of the pre-
Adamite world. Rather, he sees continuing generations of natural
people who have not sinned (as opposed to resurrected saints) popu-
lating the new earth. For a deeper study of this teaching, see the com-
mentary references under the index heading of "generations" in *The
Dake Annotated Reference Bible*.

struction by water in the past and the renovation by fire in the future indicate that twice the earth has been made perfect and inhabited, and twice the earth has failed to follow God's plan. As we have seen, the third time the earth will be made perfect is when God establishes the new heavens and new earth. A godly social system will then be established as evidenced by Peter's comment that righteousness will dwell in the new heavens and the new earth.

Part Two

RAMIFICATIONS

REINTERPRETING GENESIS 1

It is our hope that the previous chapters have demonstrated, at least somewhat persuasively, not only the possibility but the plausibility of the pre-Adamite world. We have challenged the traditional view of creation, exposing and exploring the apparent gap between the first two verses of Genesis chapter one. We have seen how the destruction of the pre-Adamite world satisfies seeming discrepancies between God's original creation "in the beginning," and the chaotic state of the earth as we find it in Genesis 1:2. And we have found that the existence and overthrow of this pre-Adamite civilization is substantiated in several passages of Scripture, many of which are fully clarified only from this perspective. In this second part of the book, we will examine further ramifications of this viewpoint.

The most obvious place to begin is with the reinterpretation of the Genesis material. Since Genesis 1:3 - 2:25 is no longer being viewed as the original creation, it must now be seen as the re-creation or restoration of the earth, following the destruction of the pre-Adamite world described in Genesis 1:2.[1]

THE STORY OF RE-CREATION

Light Restored

> And God said, Let there be light: and there was light. And God saw the light, that it was good: and God divided the light from the darkness. And God called the light Day, and the darkness he called Night. And the evening and the morning were the first day. (Gen. 1:3-5)

The work of this day was simply the restoration of light and the division of light and darkness, or the restoration of day and night on earth

---

1. Exodus 20:11 and 31:17 have often been used to prove that the six days of Genesis 1 refers to the original creation of the heavens and the earth, 6,000 years ago. Exodus 20:11 states: "For in six days the LORD made heaven and earth, the sea, and all that in them is, and rested the seventh day: wherefore the LORD blessed the sabbath day, and hallowed it." Exodus 31:17 states, "It is a sign between me and the children of Israel for ever: for in six days the LORD made heaven and earth, and on the seventh day he rested, and was refreshed." In both of these texts, however, the word "made" is the Hebrew word `asah, meaning to make out of pre-existing material. In other words, the passages refer to restoration or re-creation, not the original creation out of nothing as bara' would have indicated.

as it was when Lucifer ruled, before God cursed the earth with total darkness. This restoration came about as the Spirit of God brooded over the waters that covered the earth (v. 2), and by the direct command of God, "Let there be light."

Both light and darkness, were already in existence, having been created originally with the heavens and the earth. The command in Genesis 1:3 is the divine equivalent of "Turn on the light." Throughout Genesis 1, the idea of "let" is that of permission or command, not creation. This further indicates that the darkness of Genesis 1:2 is an act of judgment. The first day of re-creation thus involves God's permission for judgment to cease; the sun, moon, and stars are allowed to shine again on the darkened planet according to their original creative purpose.

Remember, there was a state of chaos prior to re-creation; the natural laws which previously governed the universe had been temporarily nullified because of sin. Now, in the restoration to perfection, God merely commands and the sun gives light again, as it had done throughout Lucifer's reign. Therefore, the work of the first day was simply the restoration of day and night as it had been on the pre-Adamite earth (Jer. 4:23-26; 2 Pet. 3:5-7).

Firmament Restored

And God said, Let there be a firmament in

> the midst of the waters, and let it divide the
> waters from the waters. And God made the
> firmament, and divided the waters which were
> under the firmament from the waters which
> were above the firmament: and it was so. And
> God called the firmament Heaven. And the
> evening and the morning were the second
> day. (Gen. 1:6-8)

The work of the second day was the restoration of the firmament, or the clouds, to once
again hold the waters that had fallen on the earth
to cause Lucifer's flood and destroy the first social system. These waters had been in the firmament and had been poured out as rain to water
the earth throughout the length of Lucifer's rule,
for when Satan fell he said, "I will ascend above
the heights of the clouds" (Isa. 14:12-14). These
same clouds were originally created to hold mois-
ture to water the earth (Job 38:4-9, 25-30; Ps.
104:2-3, 13-14).

In the judgment on the original creation,
the fountains of the deep combined with the condensing vapors of the heavens to flood the earth.
Because the sun was withheld from shining on
the earth, the waters could not be vaporized again
until the restoration of sunlight. Because of this,
the waters did not naturally abate from the earth
after Lucifer's flood, as they did continually in the
days of Noah (Gen. 7:24; 8:3-11). Because the
waters were then divided again as they were before the chaos of Genesis 1:2, natural laws took

care of flood conditions on earth in Noah's time. Both waters and firmament were created "in the beginning," and now were merely being restored to their original state.

The firmament then was created "in the beginning," but on the second day it was restored to its original creative purpose. This was done by *making*, not *creating*, the clouds. Genesis 2:6 tells of a mist rising from the earth which "watered the whole face of the ground." God had just finished dividing the waters, causing some to be retained by the clouds as they were before Lucifer's flood (Gen. 1:2). There would naturally be vapors and fogs rising from the earth and condensing into dew as today (Ps. 135:7; 148:8; Jer. 10:12-13). It could not mean that this is how God watered the earth for 1,656 years between Adam and Noah and that no man had ever seen it rain until after the ark was made. If so, this would nullify the very purpose for which God made the clouds.

Clouds have existed since creation to give rain on the earth. There was no rain in the six days before Adam was created and before vegetation was in the ground; but after that there was rain in season throughout the 1,656 years before Noah, as has been the case ever since.

Earth and Vegetation Restored

> And God said, Let the waters under the heaven be gathered together unto one place,

and let the dry land appear: and it was so. And
God called the dry land Earth; and the gath-
ering together of the waters called he Seas:
and God saw that it was good. And God said,
Let the earth bring forth grass, the herb yielding seed, and the fruit tree yielding fruit after
his kind, whose seed is in itself, upon the
earth: and it was so. And the earth brought
forth grass, and herb yielding seed after his
kind, and the tree yielding fruit, whose seed
was in itself, after his kind: and God saw that
it was good. And the evening and the morning were the third day. (Gen. 1:9-13)

The work of the third day included the
restoration of the earth from its water baptism
(which had lasted all through the period of chaos
and through the first two days) and the restoration of the vegetation that had grown on the earth
before the chaos of Genesis 1:2. As we have seen,
the fruitful earth had become a wasteland because
of the judgment sent for Lucifer's rebellion. But
as the psalmist describes this phase of restoration,
"At thy [God's] rebuke, they [the waters] fled; at
the voice of thy thunder they hasted away" (Ps.
104:7). In other words, the waters that hadn't
evaporated and formed clouds on the second day
were now commanded to return to the places God
originally created to contain them—basins, river
beds, and the bowels of the earth—where they
had been before being commanded to help cause
the flood of Genesis 1:2. God then set boundaries around the waters so that they would be pre-

vented from covering the earth (Ps. 104:5-9). At this point the earth could then appear as it was when it was originally created and inhabited (Gen. 1:1, 9; Isa. 45:18).

The purpose of vegetation was to sustain life on the restored earth. Apparently all seeds died during the judgment when the earth was covered with water for an indefinite period. As we have already seen, the waters from Noah's flood did not destroy vegetation, so this flood must have lasted considerably longer. Indeed, Genesis 2:4-5 plainly states "that the LORD God made [`*asah*] the earth and the heavens, and every plant of the field before it was in the earth, and every herb of the field before it grew." This proves that all vegetation was re-created on the third day.

Solar Regulation Restored

> And God said, Let there be lights in the firmament of the heaven to divide the day from the night; and let them be for signs, and for seasons, and for days, and years: and let them be for lights in the firmament of the heaven to give light upon the earth: and it was so. And God made two great lights; the greater light to rule the day, and the lesser light to rule the night: he made the stars also. And God set them in the firmament of the heaven to give light upon the earth, and to rule over the day and over the night, and to divide the light from the darkness: and God saw that it was good. And the evening and the morning were the fourth day. (Gen. 1:14-19)

The work of the fourth day was the restoration of the solar system. This logically followed
the restoration of the earth on the day before. The
two great lights were to divide day and night, regu-
lating the amount of light and darkness, as well
as the intensity of their heat and cold. Thus, they
were "for signs, and for seasons, and for days, and
years" (v. 14). Though the language here speaks
of the function of heavenly bodies, it really dem-
onstrates that the daily motion of the earth on its
axis was in operation.

As mentioned above, these lights were
made (`asah), not created (bara'). They were origi-
nally created with other parts of the universe "in
the beginning." Furthermore, they were already
present in Genesis 1:3 when God said, "Let there
be light." It is during the work of the fourth day
that the lights once again fulfill their creative
purposes in the newly restored earth.

Genesis 1:15 states that these lights were
"to give light upon the earth." They had shone
upon the waters during the first and second days,
but not upon the earth, for it was under water
until the third day. With the earth restored, the
permanent regulation of the solar system (as before the chaos of Genesis 1:2) was the next natural step.

These lights had illuminated the earth, and
had regulated times and seasons all through
Lucifer's reign, but in the judgment on the first
social system they had been withheld from shin-

ing on the cursed earth. God here commanded them to renew their original creative purpose to sustain life on earth, and to permanently regulate times and seasons and day and night.

Fish and Fowl Restored

> And God said, Let the waters bring forth abundantly the moving creature that hath life, and fowl that may fly above the earth in the open firmament of heaven. And God created great whales, and every living creature that moveth, which the waters brought forth abundantly, after their kind, and every winged fowl after his kind: and God saw that it was good. And God blessed them, saying, Be fruitful, and multiply, and fill the waters in the seas, and let fowl multiply in the earth. And the evening and the morning were the fifth day. (Gen. 1:20-23)

The work of the fifth day involved the creation and formation of new birds and marine life. This passage records the first creative act of God specifically mentioned since the original creation of the heavens and the earth described in Genesis 1:1. (Though not expressly stated as such, the new vegetation on the third day would also have been a new creation.) Everything else up till now has just been a restoration of creation to its pre-Adamite state.

But here the word *bara'* (translated "created" in v. 21) is used for the first time since verse one. All that was done in the interval was a rear-rangement and restoration of matter. Now life is introduced, which requires creative power beyond mere reconstruction. All forms of animal life in the air and in the waters are embraced in the state-ments of this verse. After restoring the realms where fish and fowl were to live, God then cre-ated them to reproduce their own kind naturally. The bodies of all living creatures were formed out of the dust of the ground, and then life was cre-ated in them (Gen. 2:19).

Every creature was to bring forth "after his kind" (Gen. 1:11-25), illustrating the law of re-production governing all things. This same law was still in force after the flood of Noah, for "ev-ery beast, every creeping thing, and every fowl, and whatsoever creepeth upon the earth, after their kinds, went forth out of the ark" (Gen. 8:19).

Land Animals and Man Restored

> And God said, Let the earth bring forth the living creature after his kind, cattle, and creep-ing thing, and beast of the earth after his kind: and it was so. And God made the beast of the earth after his kind, and cattle after their kind, and every thing that creepeth upon the earth after his kind: and God saw that it was good. And God said, Let us make man in our im-age, after our likeness: and let them have do-minion over the fish of the sea, and over the fowl of the air, and over the cattle, and over all the earth, and over every creeping thing

that creepeth upon the earth. So God created
man in his own image, in the image of God
created he him; male and female created he
them. And God blessed them, and God said
unto them, Be fruitful, and multiply, and replenish the earth, and subdue it: and have
dominion over the fish of the sea, and over
the fowl of the air, and over every living thing
that moveth upon the earth. And God said,
Behold, I have given you every herb bearing
seed, which is upon the face of all the earth,
and every tree, in the which is the fruit of a
tree yielding seed; to you it shall be for meat.
And to every beast of the earth, and to every
fowl of the air, and to every thing that creepeth
upon the earth, wherein there is life, I have
given every green herb for meat: and it was
so. And God saw every thing that he had
made, and, behold, it was very good. And the
evening and the morning were the sixth day.
(Gen. 1:24-31)

The work of the sixth day involved the creation of new land animals, followed by the creation of man. It concluded with God's commands
for the new creation. Both human and animal
bodies were formed out of the dust, and thus life
was created (Gen. 2:7, 19). Man and the animals
created on this final day were to take the place of
the inhabitants of the first social system over which
Lucifer ruled. Finally, the pre-Adamite world was
replaced by the Adamite world.

The "Let us" references throughout this
passage express the divine purpose in creation.

However, the method is not described until Genesis 2:5-25. In other words, Genesis 1 states *what* God did, and Genesis 2 states *how* He did it.

The Seventh Day of Rest

> Thus the heavens and the earth were finished, and all the host of them [i.e., all the inhabitants and creatures of all kinds in the heavens and the earth]. And on the seventh day God ended his work which he had made. And God blessed the seventh day, and sanctified it: because that in it he had rested from all his work which God created [*bara'*] and made [*`asah*]. These are the generations [family history or productions] of the heavens and of the earth when they were created, in the day that the LORD God made the earth and the heavens. (Gen. 2:1-4)

The seventh day was one of rest for God. He rested from His labors not because He needed a time of relaxation, but because His work of restoring the earth and its inhabitants was complete. He had been engaged in the process for six days and six nights and was now finished with His work.

The creative ages were concluded with this rest. They began "in the beginning," with the original perfect creation of the heavens and the earth and all things in them, over which Lucifer ruled before the destruction of the pre-Adamite world. This destruction reduced creation to the chaotic, desolate state described in Genesis 1:2.

All life perished because of Lucifer's rebellion.
God then restored the earth to perfection, creating new life to replace that which had been destroyed (Gen. 1:3 - 2:25). With the completion of
that work, God rested.

EPILOGUE TO RE-CREATION

A *Question of Time*

If God took six days to form new life out of
the chaos that was the result of Lucifer's fall, it
would stand to reason that He must have taken a
much longer time to originally bring into existence the substance out of which He formed the
universe. At some point in the dateless past God
took the material He had created, and with His
hands formed each sun, moon, star, planet, and
every creature that inhabits the vast universe. In
one day God divided the waters which covered
the earth and restored the firmament. God restored the earth and set bounds to the seas in one
day. It is therefore logical to believe that He took
a much longer period originally to bring the materials into existence and form the waters, the firmament, and the earth.

Astronomers have found billions of stars
in the Milky Way galaxy alone, and galaxies have
been found in the farthest reaches of the known
universe, many of which are hundreds of millions
of light-years across and contain hundreds of billions of stars. The Bible says that the heavens can-

not be measured and the host of heaven cannot be counted (Jer. 31:37; 33:22-25). The universe is so incredibly vast that scientists have been unable to detect its limits, yet the majority of the six days of Genesis 1-2 were focused only on the earth and its inhabitants. If it took that long just to restore the earth—one planet—to a second habitable state after the destruction of the pre-Adamite world, imagine how long God originally spent creating the entire universe!

When we speak of the six days of restoration and the creation of present life on earth, however, we can say with scriptural authority that these events occurred about 6,000 years ago. We have a detailed account of the genealogical record of Christ, and we can accurately establish a time frame for the re-creation of the earth by an analysis of the dispensations since Adam.

Why the Earth Was Restored

The earth was restored to a habitable state because it has always been God's intention for it to be inhabited: "For thus saith the Lord that created the heavens; God himself that formed the earth and made it; he hath established it, he created it not in vain [Heb. *tohuw*, a waste or desolation], he formed it to be inhabited" (Isa. 45:18). God created the material universe to be inhabited with intelligent beings to whom He could reveal Himself, and with whom He could share His goodness and all the rich blessings of life forever. So, after the destruction following the fall of Lucifer and the total rebellion of the pre-Adamite civilization, God continued with His original purpose by restoring the earth and making a new creation. And, in spite of the fact that the new creation has also rebelled, God declared in Numbers 14:21, "But as truly as I live, all the earth shall be filled with the glory of the LORD." This purpose will yet be realized, in the new heavens and the new earth of the future. God did not create the earth to turn it over to rebels, and He will yet see to it that only the meek and the righteous shall inherit the earth (Mt. 5:5; Ps. 37:9-11, 29). Thus God restored the earth from chaos and ruin to replenish it with His people so that His original purpose will finally be realized.

God's Plan for the New Social System

God's plan for the new social system was the same as it was for the first social system — for all of mankind to freely submit themselves to God as the Sovereign Lord of all creation. This means that men must dedicate themselves to that which God Himself is dedicated — those things which are for the best good of all society. Every thought, word, and deed must be directed toward the betterment of others, and men must live in complete dependence on God for their needs.

God planned to make the new creation an example to all angelic powers of the manifold wisdom of His eternal plan (Eph. 3:10-11; 1 Cor.

4:9). He planned to manifest His own grace and goodness to man and make him the ruler of all creation (Ps. 8:3-7). He planned that man should be faithful to his responsibility and continue his dominion as a result of his faithfulness. God planned for judgment according to the law if man failed. But He also planned a way of redemption.

The earth has seen the result of sin's destruction through two phases of history. Lucifer's fall resulted in the first, and Adam's sin resulted in the second. God created Adam on the sixth day of Genesis 1 to take the place of Lucifer as earth's ruler. Once having had a throne and subjects over whom he ruled, Lucifer had sinned and failed to reconcile with his Creator. Adam was then given dominion over the earth, and he would still be reigning if he hadn't sinned. God's method of reconciliation was to send the "second Adam," Jesus Christ, who would provide the means for the restoration of all creation. Christ Himself will be the third and final ruler of the earth. All things will be put under His feet and "of the increase of his government and peace there shall be no end." This kingdom will be established "with justice from henceforth even for ever" (Isa. 9:7).

Adam carried a great weight of responsibility. Under God, he was given dominion over all creation, including the charge to watch over it and protect it. God knew that Lucifer would contest man's claim of dominion, yet He permitted this in order to test the new governor of the earth.

When the Trinity conferred to make man, they said,

> Let us make man in our image, after our like-
> ness: and let them have dominion over the
> fish of the sea, and over the fowl of the air,
> and over the cattle, and over all the earth, and
> over every creeping thing that creepeth upon
> the earth. (Gen. 1:26)

And, after creating Adam and Eve,

> God blessed them, and God said unto them,
> Be fruitful, and multiply, and replenish the
> earth, and subdue it: and have dominion over
> the fish of the sea, and over the fowl of the
> air, and over every living thing that moveth
> upon the earth. (Gen. 1:28)

Adam was thus charged with the responsibility of bringing more of his kind into the world and training them to respect God, to continue in righteousness, to reject all temptation and to overcome all enemies. David described the extent of man's dominion this way:

> When I consider thy heavens, the work of thy
> fingers, the moon and the stars, which thou
> hast ordained; what is man, that thou art
> mindful of him? and the son of man, that thou
> visitest him? For thou hast made him a little
> lower than the angels, and hast crowned him
> with glory and honour. Thou madest him to
> have dominion over the works of thy hands;

> thou hast put all things under his feet: all
> sheep and oxen, yea, and the beasts of the
> field; the fowl of the air, and the fish of the
> sea, and whatsoever passeth through the paths
> of the seas. (Ps. 8:3-8)

From these and other passages we learn
that God's plan for man was that he should have
dominion over everything. What a great responsibility! What a great position! Man was fully ca-
pable of ruling over all things, for his intellect
had not yet been corrupted by the fall, and as a
result was able to name everything in creation.
But man sinned and came "short of the glory of
God" (Rom. 3:23).

Scripture tells us that in the final restoration of all things the resurrected saints will again
have dominion and will help God administer the
affairs of the universe (Rev. 1:5-6; 2:26-29; 3:21;
5:8-10; 22:4-5; 1 Cor. 6:2-3; 2 Tim. 2:12). Paul
expresses this beautifully:

> The Spirit himself testifies with our spirit that
> we are God's children. Now if we are chil-
> dren, then we are heirs—heirs of God and
> co-heirs with Christ, if indeed we share in his
> sufferings in order that we may also share in
> his glory (Rom. 8:16-17, NIV).

Everything that God owns will become the inheritance of the saints, and they shall reign forever and ever (Rev. 1:5-6; 2:27; 5:9-10; 22:4-5; Dan.
7:13-14, 18, 27).

What a future awaits those who follow the Lord! A brief glimpse of God's eternal plan for man should cause all mankind to wholeheartedly surrender to God and conform to His eternal will. But because the enemy keeps people occupied with petty, temporal things; and because they so easily lose sight of their eternal future, people neglect God and are cut off from their potential inheritance in Christ. But God will carry on His eternal purposes with those who choose to take part in His plan for man.

Chapter 8 _____

THE DATELESS PAST

As we've stated, the second part of this book deals with some of the results of believing in the pre-Adamite world. In other words, once the theory has been proven and (hopefully) accepted, what impact does it have on our other beliefs? This question represents a "front door" approach to the ramifications of our view of creation. It embraces immediate concerns; it anticipates logical consequences and tackles them "head on." The reinterpretation of the Genesis account handled in the previous chapter was clearly a "front door" approach. But where there is a front door, there is usually a back door as well. In our case, there is more than one.

Going through the front door means facing problems that arise as a direct result of challenging tradition. The "back door" approach is somewhat different. It takes pre-existing problems and shows how the new concept solves them. In this chapter, the pre-existing problems have to do with the dateless past. Namely, what did God do in eternity past, before creation? The logical problems posed by this question exist only if the traditional view of creation is maintained. They are resolved when we accept that God's work during the six days of Genesis 1-2 was that of restoration rather than original creation.

The Eternity of God

Though the Scriptures tell us all we need to know to walk with God and get to heaven, they don't tell us everything there is to know. In other words, the Bible is complete, but it's not exhaustive. Speaking of the works of Jesus, John closes his gospel by saying "that even the world itself could not contain the books that should be written" (John 21:25). If such is true of the brief earthly life of Christ, how much more does it describe the vast account of God's acts in eternity past? Indeed, there are untold mysteries, as Moses states in Deuteronomy 29:29, "The secret things belong unto the LORD our God: but those things which are revealed belong unto us and to our children for ever, that we may do all the words of this law."

One thing we are certain of, however, is that God has existed from eternity: "Before the mountains were brought forth, or ever Thou hadst formed the earth and the world, even from ever-lasting to everlasting, Thou art God" writes Moses in Psalm 90:2. David echoes this sentiment, say-ing, "Thy throne is established of old: Thou art from everlasting" (Ps. 93:2). In his personification of wisdom, Solomon declares, "The LORD brought me forth as the first of his works, before his deeds of old; I was appointed from eternity, from the beginning, before the world began" (Pr. 8:22-23, NIV). Prophesying of the birth of Christ, Micah describes Him as one "whose goings forth have been from of old, from everlasting" (Mic. 5:2). Expressing himself in timeless language, John writes, "In the beginning was the Word, and the Word was with God, and the Word was God. The same was in the beginning with God" (John 1:1-2). Consequently, John's Revelation bears greet-ings "from him who is, and who was, and who is to come" (Rev. 1:4, NIV), whom the four beasts worship, "saying, Holy, holy, holy is the Lord God Almighty, who was, and is, and is to come" (Rev. 4:8, NIV). And, just in case we didn't quite get the point, He reminds us: "I am Alpha and Omega, the beginning and the end, the first and the last" (Rev. 22:13).

Eternity is simply beyond human compre-hension. When attempting to explain the con-cept of God's eternal nature to children, one of the first questions they ask is, "What did God do for all that time? Wouldn't He get bored?"

Well, we know this about God: He loves

to create. So significant is His creative activity that He has chosen Creator as one of His titles. Through the mouthpiece of Isaiah, God asks,

> "To whom will you compare me? Or who is my equal?" says the Holy One. Lift your eyes and look to the heavens: who created all these? He who brings out the starry host one by one, and calls them each by name. Because of his great power and mighty strength, not one of them is missing. Why do you say, O Jacob, and complain, O Israel, "My way is hidden from the LORD; my cause is disregarded by my God"? Do you not know? Have you not heard? The LORD is the everlasting God, the Creator of the ends of the earth. He will not grow tired or weary, and his understanding no one can fathom. He gives strength to the weary and increases the power of the weak. Even youths grow tired and weary, and young men stumble and fall; but those who hope in the LORD will renew their strength. They will soar on wings like eagles; they will run and not grow weary, they will walk and not be faint. (Isa. 40:25-31, NIV; cf. Isa. 43:15)

God's role as Creator thus conveys an image of incredible, tireless strength. For this reason, Peter uses the title to encourage suffering Christians: "Wherefore let them that suffer according to the will of God commit the keeping of their souls to him in well doing, as unto a faithful Creator" (1 Pet. 4:19). And Paul, who finds it unthinkably heinous to sin against such a majestic Being, exposes the depraved behavior of those "who changed the truth of God into a lie, and worshipped and served the creature more than the Creator, who is blessed for ever" (Rom. 1:25).

We also know that creation brings God pleasure. As the twenty-four elders fall prostrate and "worship him that liveth for ever and ever," they "cast their crowns before the throne" and declare, "Thou art worthy, O Lord, to receive glory and honour and power: for thou hast created all things, and for thy pleasure they are and were created" (Rev. 4:10-11). Part of that pleasure must be the joy of revealing Himself to His creation. As David proclaims,

> The heavens declare the glory of God; the skies proclaim the work of his hands. Day after day they pour forth speech; night after night they display knowledge. There is no speech or language where their voice is not heard. Their voice goes out into all the earth, their words to the ends of the world. (Ps. 19:1-4, NIV)

According to Paul, this ongoing revelation of God in nature is so powerful that men are held accountable for the truth they receive about God through creation itself:

> The wrath of God is being revealed from heaven against all the godlessness and wickedness of men who suppress the truth by their wickedness, since what may be known about God is plain to them, because God has made

it plain to them. For since the creation of the world God's invisible qualities—his eternal power and divine nature—have been clearly seen, being understood from what has been made, so that men are without excuse. (Rom. 1:18-20, NIV)

Through the Back Door

Now, stop and think for just a moment. We've seen that God is eternal. As impossible as it is for us to conceive, He had no beginning. He is the One whose name is I AM (Ex. 3:14). And yet He is the Creator who delights in revealing Himself through His creation. But if the traditional understanding of creation is to be believed, then we have a picture of God waiting through countless eons to create the heavens and the earth for the first time a mere 6,000 years ago. Are we really to believe that Adam was the first man to whom God revealed Himself?

John tells us twice that "God is love" (1 Jn. 4:8, 16). It stands to reason then that since God is eternal, His love must also be eternal. Indeed, this is just what Jeremiah records when he expresses God's heart to Israel: "I have loved thee with an everlasting love: therefore with lovingkindness have I drawn thee" (Jer. 31:3). The Hebrew word translated "everlasting" here is *olam*. Found over 400 times in Scripture, *olam* means eternal, perpetual, continuous; time without end. It is used to speak of God's "everlasting covenant" (Gen. 9:16; 17:7, 13, 19; 2 Sam. 23:5), and of the fact that He is an "everlasting God" (Gen. 21:33). When Moses asked God what name he should use to tell Israel about the God of their fathers, God answered with "I AM THAT I AM," saying, "Thus shalt thou say unto the children of Israel, I AM hath sent me unto you" (Ex. 3:14). In the next verse, God said, "this is my name for ever [olam]" (Ex. 3:15). In the midst of his song of victory, Moses declared, "The LORD shall reign for ever [olam] and ever" (Ex. 15:18; cf. Ps. 9:7; 10:16; 29:10). David expressed the Old Testament promise of eternal life by saying, "Depart from evil, and do good; and dwell for evermore [olam]. For the LORD loveth judgment, and forsaketh not his saints; they are preserved for ever [olam]" (Ps. 37:27-28).

In Jeremiah 31:3, "I have loved thee" is in the perfect tense. Combined with the power of olam to modify God's "everlasting love," we get a picture of a love that has been in God's heart for a *really* long time. So we have a God who has existed throughout all eternity past; a God who is love and whose love for man is everlasting; and He is a God who loves to Create and reveal Himself through creation. In light of all this, how can we believe that with all of eternity to work with, God's first creative act was 6,000 years ago? "In the beginning," on the other hand, could have been any length of time in the dateless past. And we have no specified time limits whatsoever for the length of the pre-Adamite civilization prior to

Lucifer's fall.

Admittedly, it reflects our limited human perspective to measure time in this way, for we know that God does not view time like we do. Moses wrote that "a thousand years in thy sight are but as yesterday when it is past, and as a watch in the night" (Ps. 90:4). Peter borrowed this theme in 2 Peter 3:8, saying that "one day is with the Lord as a thousand years, and a thousand years as one day." The point is simply to show that in addition to all the biblical evidence for the pre-Adamite world, there is also a compelling logic to the concept. It stands to reason that the original creation "in the beginning" took place over 6,000 years ago.

Chapter 9 _____

A PIVOTAL DOCTRINE

As we've already seen, the traditional view of the creation account in Genesis has been sustained by the rather ambiguous rendering of *tohuw va bohuw* as "without form, and void." Yet a thorough examination of the original language and its usage throughout Scripture has exposed the flaws of the traditional view and pointed us toward an understanding of a pre-Adamite world existing and being overthrown between the first two verses of Genesis. Similarly, there is a phrase in the New Testament that is generally understood in a way which belies its true meaning. And, once again, the most common interpretation is that of original creation, when in reality, the expression points to the overthrow of the pre-Adamite world.

"The foundation of the world" occurs ten

times in the New Testament. Every time it combines the same two Greek words, *katabole* (rendered "foundation") and *kosmos* (rendered "world"). As we studied in chapter six, while the word *kosmos* occasionally refers to the physical world, its primary meaning as used in Scripture is that of social order. Hence, we already have reason to suspect the traditional interpretation of this phrase. As we press on, that suspicion will grow into certainty.

Two Greek Words: Themelios *and* Katabole

Of the 27 times the word "foundation" occurs in the New Testament, only 10 times is it a translation of *katabole*, all 10 being in the phrase "the foundation of the world." The Greek word *themelios* accounts for the remaining occurrences, with the exception of Hebrews 1:10, where the phrase "hast laid the foundation" comes from the verb form, *themelioo*. As we examine the verses containing *themelios*, we will discover that its meaning is quite clear.

Themelios

This word makes its first appearance in Luke 6:48 where Jesus is explaining what the man is like who hears His sayings and does them:

> He is like a man which built an house, and digged deep, and laid the foundation [*themelios*] on a rock: and when the flood arose, the stream beat vehemently upon that

house, and could not shake it: for it was
founded [*themelioo*] upon a rock.

By way of contrast,

he that heareth, and doeth not, is like a man
that without a foundation [*themelios*] built an
house upon the earth; against which the
stream did beat vehemently, and immediately
it fell; and the ruin of that house was great.
(Lk. 6:49)

Jesus again uses the picture of construction to
teach on the cost of discipleship:

For which of you, intending to build a tower,
sitteth not down first, and counteth the cost,
whether he have sufficient to finish it? Lest
haply, after he hath laid the foundation
[*themelios*], and is not able to finish it, all that
behold it begin to mock him, saying, This
man began to build, and was not able to finish. (Lk. 14:28-30)

When Paul and Silas worshipped at midnight, an
earthquake shook "the foundations of the prison"
(Acts 16:26). By faith, Abraham "looked for a city
which hath foundations, whose builder and maker
is God" (Heb. 11:10). While imprisoned on
Patmos, John saw such a city:

And the wall of the city had twelve foundations [*themelios*], and in them the names of
the twelve apostles of the Lamb. . . . And the

> foundations [*themelios*] of the wall of the city
> were garnished with all manner of precious
> stones. The first foundation was jasper; the
> second, sapphire; the third, a chalcedony; the
> fourth, an emerald; the fifth, sardonyx; the
> sixth, sardius; the seventh, chrysolite; the
> eighth, beryl; the ninth, a topaz; the tenth, a
> chrysoprasus; the eleventh, a jacinth; the
> twelfth, an amethyst. (Rev. 21:14, 19-20).

With such powerful physical imagery, it's easy to see how *themelios* lends itself to metaphorical descriptions of life in Christ. Because of Paul's pioneering spirit as an apostle to the Gentiles, it was not his desire to "build upon another man's foundation" (Rom. 15:20), but he fully expected others to follow after him:

> According to the grace of God which is given
> unto me, as a wise masterbuilder, I have laid
> the foundation [*themelios*], and another
> buildeth thereon. But let every man take heed
> how he buildeth thereupon. For other foun-
> dation [*themelios*] can no man lay than that
> is laid, which is Jesus Christ. Now if any man
> build upon this foundation [*themelios*] gold,
> silver, precious stones, wood, hay, stubble;
> every man's work shall be made manifest: for
> the day shall declare it, because it shall be
> revealed by fire; and the fire shall try every
> man's work of what sort it is. (1 Cor. 3:10-13)

From the above study, we can easily see that *themelios* is the standard Greek word for "foundation" in the sense in which we commonly use the term. Interestingly, the verb form *themelioo* is also used once in the same sense that is traditionally applied to expression "the foundation of the world." Hebrews 1:10 reads, "And, Thou, Lord, in the beginning hast laid the foundation [*themelioo*] of the earth; and the heavens are the works of thine hands." Here, in this obviously creation-oriented text, we have the standard term for "foundation," and the common word for the physical earth, *ge*, rightly translated "earth" 188 times in the New Testament.

If *katabole* and *kosmos* were perfectly synonymous with *themelios* and *ge* respectively, then there would be no problems with the traditional understanding of "the foundation of the world." But this is not the case. As we've already seen, the primary meaning of *kosmos* in the New Testament is not in the planetary sense (as is the case with *ge*); rather, it means "world" in the sense of social system. So the question remains, what does *katabole* really mean?

Katabole

As we've mentioned, all ten occurrences of the noun *katabole* are in the phrase "the foundation of the world." Since we already know that *kosmos* means social system, it's immediately doubtful that this expression has a creation orientation. A study of the root of *katabole* will confirm these doubts.

Katabole comes from the verb *kataballo* which means to cast down. Paul, speaking of the power of God at work in him to overcome the attacks of the enemy, triumphantly announces the victory of those who are "persecuted, but not forsaken; cast down [*kataballo*], but not destroyed" (2 Cor. 4:9). And again, John hears the proclamation from heaven that "Now is come salvation, and strength, and the kingdom of our God, and the power of his Christ: for the accuser of our brethren is cast down [*kataballo*], which accused them before our God day and night" (Rev. 12:10). When this verbal idea is expressed as a noun, the concept of "ruin" or "overthrow" is far more natural than that of "foundation."

Overthrow of the Pre-Adamite Social System

Therefore, knowing that *katabole* means overthrow and *kosmos* refers to a social system, "the foundation of the world" becomes "the overthrow of the social system." And the only social system that has been completely overthrown thus far is that of the pre-Adamite world. Consequently, all ten references to "foundation of the world" are really references to the overthrow of the pre-Adamite social system.

This is especially significant when we consider that only two prepositions are used to modify the phrase "foundation of the world." Seven of the ten occurrences of the phrase are modified by the Greek preposition *apo*, almost always translated "from" in the KJV. The root idea of *apo* is that of separation, and temporal separation is one of its meanings. In the temporal sense then, *apo* carries the meaning of an event separated from its origin by a length of time. In that case, "*since the overthrow of the social system*" is a more accurate interpretation of this phrase. The three remaining uses of "the foundation of the world" are modified by the Greek preposition *pro* which has the sense of previous or prior. Hence, it is rightly translated "before."

What we have then is a phrase that expresses a pivotal event in history, with significant facts dated either *before* it or *after* it. With this in mind, let's consider the passages where "foundation of the world" occurs, treating the texts that include *pro* first.

Before (Pro) the Overthrow

In His great high-priestly prayer, Jesus said, "Father, I will that they also, whom thou hast given me, be with me where I am; that they may behold my glory, which thou hast given me: for thou lovedst me before the foundation of the world." In other words, Jesus reveals His eternal coexistence with the Father and the love they shared as Father and Son, long before the destruction of the pre-Adamite world.

We see this same usage very clearly in Paul's writings, despite the fact that he was in no way concerned with outlining a chronology of creation events. In the New Testament passage we're going to look at, he was much more concerned with delineating God's incredible redemptive plan. Christ's work is the focus here, and any allusion to a world created before Adam is included only as a means to clarify and expand on God's plan for man.

Paul barely takes time to greet the church at Ephesus before praises begin to leap from his lips as he revels in God's unimaginable redemptive plan. In the first fourteen verses Paul joyfully reminds us that God has blessed us with all spiritual blessings; chosen us in Christ to be holy; predestined us to be adopted as children; made us accepted in the beloved; redeemed and forgiven us by the blood of Christ; abounded toward us in all wisdom; made known to us His will; given us an inheritance; and sealed us unto the day of redemption. The apostle clearly states that this incredible plan was in the mind of God even before the judgment that was pronounced over the pre-Adamite world.

Our focus is on the fourth verse where Paul makes reference to the destruction of a world before Adam: "According as he hath chosen us in him before the foundation of the world, that we should be holy and without blame before him in love" (Eph. 1:4). In this passage the apostle teaches that even as far back as "before the foundation [destruction, overthrow] of the world [*kosmos*, social order]," God planned to restore the earth and provide redemption through Christ, should the new creation fail. For this reason, Peter states that Christ "was foreordained before the foundation of the world" (1 Pet. 1:20), or before the pre-Adamite world was destroyed, as God looked ahead to future redemption of the next social system.

Since (Apo) the Overthrow

The above passages express truths that are temporally immeasurable, things that were in the heart of God sometime in the dateless past, before the destruction of the pre-Adamite world. The following texts modified by *apo* reveal things subsequent to this cataclysmic event.

Matthew explained Jesus' ministry of teaching in parables, saying that it was to fulfill the Messianic prophecy, "I will open my mouth in parables; I will utter things which have been kept secret from the foundation of the world" (Mt. 13:35). Jesus spoke of a time when those blessed by His Father would be invited to inherit the kingdom prepared for them "from the foundation of the world" (Mt. 25:34). In His great "woe" to the lawyers, Jesus spoke of "the blood of all the prophets, which was shed from the foundation of the world" (Lk. 11:50). The writer of Hebrews, whom we believe to be Paul, said that if Christ's priesthood had been like the Levitical priesthood, then He would have had to suffer often "since the foundation of the world" (Heb. 9:26, where *apo* is rightly translated "since"). On the contrary, He suffered only once to atone for the sin of the second social order on earth. That is, Christ came to redeem Adam and his descendants, who were created since the overthrow of Lucifer and those over whom he ruled.

We see this, perhaps more clearly, in the book of Revelation. Part of John's panoramic vision includes references to the book of life, which he mentions six times. In Revelation 17:8 John alludes to a time frame for those whose names have been written in the book of life "from the foundation of the world," or since the overthrow of the pre-Adamite social system. Why would there have been a book of life before Adam himself was created? It would have had no purpose for Adam and his race if they had never rebelled against their Creator. According to this passage, the book of life was prepared for those descendants of Adam who have since chosen to take advantage of God's redemptive plan. There is no reference to a book of life for the pre-Adamite race. We don't know what means of redemption God had in store for them, but we do know that God had a plan for the descendants of Adam that involved Christ's work on the cross, a plan that would provide a means of redemption for a world not yet fallen. As a result, we see that since the overthrow of the pre-Adamite social system, each person has his name written in the book of life when he is born again and goes through the process of adoption as a child into the family of God.

In the letter to the Hebrews we find one of the strongest statements in Scripture that the six days' work of Genesis 1:3 - 2:25 occurred after the overthrow of the pre-Adamite world:

> For we which have believed do enter into rest, as he said, As I have sworn in my wrath, if they shall enter into my rest: although *the works were finished from the foundation of the world.* For he spake in a certain place of the seventh day on this wise, And God did rest the seventh day from all his works. (Heb. 4:3-4, emphasis added)

Here Paul plainly states that God finished His works after the overthrow of the first social system. The works mentioned in this passage could not be the original creation of the heavens and the earth of Genesis 1:1, but must refer to the six days of re-creation in Genesis 1:3 - 2:25, for Paul clearly dates God's rest on "the seventh day."

We can see very clearly, therefore, that the overthrow of the pre-Adamite social system is an event forming a great dividing line between the ages. This line is drawn between the dateless past when Lucifer ruled the earth and the present time during which man has been given dominion of the earth. This event thus separates the administration of the earth by angels and man's administration of the earth.

RESOLVING THE TENSION

Faith and science have not always been at odds with each other. For the authors of Scripture, the creation was a manifestation of God Himself, and His personality could be seen in the things He had made. In his letter to the Romans, Paul says that "the invisible things of him from the creation of the world are clearly seen, being understood by the things that are made" (Rom. 1:20). Paul maintains that nature is impregnated with manifestations of the attributes of God, including His omnipotence and deity. In fact, because nature so clearly reflects the personality of the Creator, Paul argues that those who reject God are left "without excuse."

The possibility that this kind of unity could exist between faith and science appears foolish to those of us standing at the doorway to the twenty-first century. The two have been, if not mutually exclusive, at least antagonistically opposed to one another for such a long time. Those who have held fast to a literal interpretation of the Scriptures have been on the defensive for at least the past hundred years. And it's taken a toll. Many Christians are afraid to grapple with the issue, apprehensive that their faith may not withstand the barrage of scientific evidence aimed at undermining the foundations of their belief system. Others attempt to explain away the vast accumulation of scientific evidence gathered during the past century. But in so doing they build mansions of glass which are easily shattered by the smallest stone casually tossed at the fragile framework of their cosmology.

In this book we've tried to find another answer. The Bible really does have something to say about the earth's origins. It gives us a secure foundation upon which to build our understanding of the universe. As Christians we don't have to be afraid of the ramifications of the next scientific discovery. We can face the secular world head-on, secure in the knowledge that what science has to say only helps us understand a little more of the nature and character of the Creator.

This book was not intended to be scientific treatise, but on the other hand it is not set in an oppositional stance to the claims of science. If, as Paul says, the personality of God is reflected in nature, then faith and science should walk hand-in-hand. What we read in the Scriptures concerning creation events should line up with what science tells us about the earth's history. If that's true, then what's gone wrong?

The New Role of Science

The scientific method found its roots in the understanding that the Creator had fashioned the universe in an infinitely intricate pattern, a pattern in which order could be discovered and understood. From these beginnings, history has witnessed a transition as science, once the handmaid of faith, took on the role of ultimate arbiter of truth. Science became the measure of reality, forming the grid through which man could understand the world around him.

Where nature once pointed us towards the Creator, science has redirected our gaze. Where once we looked through the window of Scripture to understand the world in which we live, we now peer through the lens of a microscope. And where science and Scripture seem to conflict, science has taken on the task of redefining and reinter-preting God's message to conform to its own stan-dards. The result is that our vision of the God who formed the heavens with nothing more than a word has become distant and vague.

Is science really to blame for our inability to find God? Not at all. We maintain that science as a discipline is vital to our understanding of the universe. Indeed, it reflects the majesty of the Creator that man is so highly motivated to search and discover the truth about the world in which he lives. The real problem is when God is removed from the equation and the authority of His Word is usurped.

Returning to the Authority of Scripture

It is only when we take the Word of God as our frame of reference that we can understand the world in which we live. With Scripture as our foundation, we not only have a solid footing upon which to build, we have the brick and mortar with which to erect structures that will withstand the tests of time.

And that's where the tension between faith and science finds resolution. We must let the Bible, the source of ultimate truth, guide us in our discoveries. Whether our investigations take us into the natural realm or into Scripture itself, the Word of God should be the lamp that throws its light to illumine our steps.

This has been our goal—to let Scripture lead us in our exploration of the creation narrative. Laying aside our preconceived ideas and long-held notions and gazing into God's Word with expectancy, we can find truths previously hidden. If we glance back through the material we've covered, we'll find that this journey through the Scriptures has taken us to new and exciting places. We've allowed the panorama of biblical history to unfold before us and we've discovered in the process that science falls in line with what we've read on the pages of God's Word. Along the way, the tension between faith and science has dissolved.

APPENDIX

APPENDIX A

The following material was originally a list of proofs for the pre-Adamite world in *The Dake Annotated Reference Bible*. Our first impression was that since most of this information had been expounded upon at length in the book you just read, it would be redundant. We reconsidered, however, and thought the material would make a nice summary of the main points of our argument.

1. We have a record of the original creation of the heavens and the earth in Genesis 1:1. The following facts make it clear that the term "in the beginning" used in Genesis 1:1 does not refer to the time or work of the six days of Genesis 1:3 - 2:25:

   (a) "And the earth was without form, and

void." The Hebrew word *hayah* is richer than the simple "was" would imply. *Hayah* is not a static verb, but suggests the process of becoming, indicating that the earth became waste and empty since its original creation and habitation "in the beginning."

(b)   The phrase "without form" in verse two is from the Hebrew *tohuw*, meaning waste or desolation. It is translated "waste" (Dt. 32:10); "without form" (Gen. 1:2; Jer. 4:23); "vain" (Isa. 45:18; 1 Sam. 12:21); "confusion" (Isa. 24:10; 34:11; 41:29); "empty" (Job 26:7); "vanity" (Isa. 40:17, 23; 44:9; 59:4); "nothing" (Job 6:18; Isa. 40:17); and "wilderness" (Job 12:24; Ps. 107:40). According to Isa. 45:18, God did not originally create the earth in such a waste and ruined condition, yet this is exactly the condition of the earth in Genesis 1:2. The logical conclusion, therefore, is that the earth was originally created in a perfect state, and that later it became a wasteland because of sin (Dt. 32:4; Eccl. 3:11).

(c)   The Hebrew for "void" is *bohuw*, empty, ruin, void. It is translated "void" (Gen. 1:2; Jer. 4:23); and "emptiness" (Isa. 34:11). The Hebrew phrase *tohuw va bohuw*, "waste and empty," describes the chaotic condition of the earth at the time it was cursed and flooded because of the sins of Lucifer and the pre-Adamites. It could not refer to the earth as originally created.

(d)   Throughout the Old Testament, the Hebrew word *bara'*, to create, indicates new or original creation, bringing things into existence without the use of pre-existing material. `Asah, on the other hand, primarily expresses the idea of appointment or accomplishment. Thus, we can see clearly in the following passage that God did not originally create the earth "in vain," or "without form" as it is described in Genesis 1:2:

> For thus saith the Lord that created (*bara'*) the heavens; God himself that formed the earth and made (`*asah*) it; He hath established it, He created (*bara'*) it not in vain (*tohuw*), He formed it to be inhabited: I am the Lord; and there is none else (Isaiah 45:18).

2. The earth was created to be inhabited according to Isaiah 45:18, and was inhabited before the flood of Genesis 1:2 and the work of the six days of Adam's time (Gen. 1:3 - 2:25; Isa. 14:12-14; Jer. 4:23-26; Ezek. 28:11-17; 2 Pet. 3:5-7).

3. We have the fact recorded in Genesis 1:2 that the earth, the waters, and the darkness were already in existence before the work of the six days which began in Genesis 1:3 and continued until the earth was restored to a second habitable state in Genesis 2:25. Thus, it is clear from Genesis 1:1-2 (and related scriptures) that:

(a) In the beginning—the dateless past, not six days about 6,000 years ago—God created the heavens, including the sun, moon, and stars.

(b) At the same time, God created the earth or dry land.

(c) Both the heavens and the earth were created before the earth was flooded.

(d) The earth was created dry land, not wet and flooded (vv. 1, 10; Isa. 45:18).

(e) The waters that flooded the dry land were created in the beginning along with the earth, to cause the dry land to become productive (Job 38:4-30), and not to curse the earth as in Genesis 1:2.

(f) Just the earth was cursed, flooded, and filled with darkness, not the heavens (v. 2).

4. We see in Genesis 1:2 that the Spirit of God began to move upon the earth, which was shrouded in darkness and buried under a great flood. The Spirit's purpose was restoration of life, further indicating the possibility of a pre-Adamite world destroyed then re-created during the six days of Genesis 1:3 - 2:25.

5. In Scripture, every time the sun is obscured resulting in darkness, and every time floods cover the earth, judgment for sin is the cause. Darkness and flooding are never linked with creation (Gen. 6:8 - 8:22; Ex. 10:21-23; Isa. 5:30; Jer. 4:23-26). Furthermore, every prediction of future darkness is a metaphor for a literal judgment (Mt. 8:12; 24:29-31; Rev. 6:12-17; 8:12; 9:2; 16:10; Isa. 13:10; Joel 2:30 - 3:16; Amos 5:18-20). Knowing these facts, it is certainly difficult to claim that Genesis 1:2 is an exception and the only place in Scripture where darkness and universal flooding are not acts of judgment.

6. Moses, inspired by God, recorded God's command to Adam to multiply and replenish the earth. If not a proof, this is at least an indication that there may have been a social system on the earth before Adam, for he could not *replenish* something that had not been *plenished* beforehand (Gen. 1:28). Some argue that the Hebrew word for "replenish" means "fill" and not "refill," but this is at best an argument from silence. Where the Hebrew *mala'* is translated "fill," it does not imply that the thing referred to had never been filled before. When God said to Noah, "Be fruitful, and multiply, and replenish the earth" (Gen. 9:1), it is clear that the earth had been filled before, so why not believe that God meant the same thing when He said it to Adam? The same Hebrew statement is found in both passages (Gen. 1:28; 9:1), and it is translated exactly the same in English.

7. The fact that Lucifer had already ruled the earth and become a fallen creature before Adam's time strongly suggests that Adam and his race were not the first ones on earth. We are required to acknowledge that Satan's fall was before Adam's time because he was already a fallen creature when he came into Adam's Eden (Gen. 3; 2 Cor. 11:3).

8. According to Isa. 14:12-14, Lucifer actually invaded heaven from earth, hoping to defeat God and usurp control of His kingdom. However, Lucifer himself was defeated and his kingdom

cursed. Before his defeat he had a throne and by implication must have had a kingdom and subjects over whom he ruled. His kingdom was under the clouds, under the stars, and under heaven—therefore, on earth. Having weakened the nations, and wanting to be like God and take His place in heaven, Lucifer led the invasion of heaven. All this had to be accomplished before Adam's day, for no such things have occurred, or could have occurred, since Adam was created.

9. In Ezekiel 28:11-17 we have a picture of Lucifer before he fell, as the anointed cherub or protector of the earth, full of wisdom and perfect in beauty. Ezekiel gives us a picture of Lucifer, created by God and perfect in his ways until his fall, exercising rulership and dominion over nations before Adam's day. The prophet not only states the reason for Lucifer's fall, but gives an account of the result as well. The only time these things were true of Satan was before the days of Adam.

10. In Jeremiah 4:23-26 we have a vivid description of the earth under a curse, as in Genesis 1:2. It was desolate and empty, the heavens had no light, the hills and mountains were undergoing convulsions, there was no man, no bird, no animal, no fruitful place, and no city left standing because of God's fierce anger. Jeremiah's vision of the earth could only have coincided with the record Moses gives us in Genesis 1:2. For there has never been a time from Adam's day until the

present when the earth was in such a state (not even at the time of Noah's flood). The only time Jeremiah 4:23-26 could have been fulfilled was before Adam's creation, for the earth was in such a condition when the Spirit began the six days' work of restoring it to a second habitable state (Gen. 1:2-21). Regarding the future, such will never be the condition of the earth again, for when Christ returns He will reign over all nations on earth forever, and of His kingdom there shall be no end (Gen. 8:22; 9:12; Isa. 9:6-7; 59:21; Dan. 2:44-45; 7:13-14, 18, 27; Zech. 14; Lk. 1:32-33; Rev. 1:6; 5:10; 11:15; 20:4-10; 22:4-5). Even the renovation of heaven and earth at the end of the Millennium will not make the earth desolate as pictured in Genesis 1:2 and Jeremiah 4:23-26. Therefore, Jeremiah 4:23-26 must refer to the same judgment as pictured in Genesis 1:2.

11. Psalm 104:5-9 speaks of God sending a flood on the earth after its creation, at which time the waters stood above the mountains. Verse 7 identifies this as Lucifer's flood, with the statement "At thy rebuke they fled." In the case of Noah's flood, the waters slowly and naturally abated. Furthermore, verse 9 makes it clear that this flood occurred when God set a boundary for the waters, and that is exactly what happened in the six days' work of Genesis 1:3 - 2:25. Thus, Psalm 104:5-9 must refer to the same flood as Genesis 1:2 and suggests the existence of a pre-Adamite world which was overthrown by a flood.

12. Turning to the New Testament we find that Jesus taught the fall of Satan from heaven in Luke 10:18. When did he fall? It must have been before Adam's time, for he was already a fallen creature when he came into Adam's Eden (Gen. 3). Why did he fall? Because of pride and the desire to exalt his earthly kingdom above God's (Isa. 14:12-16; Ezek. 28:11-17). What was the result of his fall? All of Satan's earthly subjects as well as over one-third of God's own angels fell with him (Rev. 12:3, 7-12); and all nations were totally destroyed, along with vegetation, fish, fowls, and animals (2 Pet. 3:5-7). Thus, Luke 10:18 substantiates the teaching of Old Testament passages regarding a pre-Adamite world.

13. Paul taught the overthrow of the pre-Adamite world (Eph. 1:4; Heb. 4:3; 9:26). In Colossians 1:15-18 he spoke of thrones, principalities, and powers in heaven and in earth, visible and invisible. Apparently, Lucifer was given one of these thrones and a kingdom before he fell. That his kingdom was on earth is indicated by the fact that he returned to the earth after his fall and, moved with envy and jealousy, brought about the downfall of the new ruler of the earth — Adam. What would motivate Lucifer to usurp man's dominion on earth if the earth was not previously Lucifer's place of rulership? Even his eternal punishment will be in the lake of fire under the earth, which further indicates that his sin must have been in connection with the earth.

APPENDIX B

The following material essentially comes from "The Dispensational Plan of God from Eternity through Eternity," found on pp. 77-78 of Dake's book, *God's Plan For Man*:

God exists in the eternal past:
Thy throne is established of old: thou art from everlasting. (Ps. 93:2)

Drafting of God's plan:
God, who at sundry times and in divers manners spake in time past unto the fathers by the prophets, Hath in these last days spoken unto us by his Son, whom he hath appointed heir of all things, by whom also he made the worlds; Who being the brightness of his glory, and the express image of his person, and upholding all things by the word of his power,

when he had by himself purged our sins, sat
down on the right hand of the Majesty on high;
Being made so much better than the angels,
as he hath by inheritance obtained a more
excellent name than they. For unto which of
the angels said he at any time, Thou art my
Son, this day have I begotten thee? And again,
I will be to him a Father, and he shall be to me
a Son? And again, when he bringeth in the
firstbegotten into the world, he saith, And let
all the angels of God worship him. And of the
angels he saith, Who maketh his angels spirits, and his ministers a flame of fire. But unto
the Son he saith, Thy throne, O God, is for
ever and ever: a sceptre of righteousness is the
sceptre of thy kingdom. (Heb. 1:1-8)

Creation of the heavens:

In the beginning God created the heaven and
the earth. (Gen. 1:1)

Creation of the spirit world:

Where wast thou when I laid the foundations
of the earth? declare, if thou hast understanding. Who hath laid the measures thereof, if
thou knowest? or who hath stretched the line
upon it? Whereupon are the foundations
thereof fastened? or who laid the corner stone
thereof; When the morning stars sang together, and all the sons of God shouted for
joy? (Job 38:4-7)

Creation of the earth — the earth made perfect the first time:

For thus saith the LORD that created the heavens; God himself that formed the earth and made it; he hath established it, he created it not in vain, he formed it to be inhabited: I am the LORD; and there is none else. (Isa. 45:18)

Creation of "the world (*kosmos*, social order) that then was":

For this they willingly are ignorant of, that by the word of God the heavens were of old, and the earth standing out of the water and in the water: Whereby the world that then was, being overflowed with water, perished: But the heavens and the earth, which are now, by the same word are kept in store, reserved unto fire against the day of judgment and perdition of ungodly men. (2 Pet. 3:5-7)

Lucifer's reign over "the world that then was"(length of reign unknown):

How art thou fallen from heaven, O Lucifer, son of the morning! how art thou cut down to the ground, which didst weaken the nations! For thou hast said in thine heart, I will ascend into heaven, I will exalt my throne above the stars of God: I will sit also upon the mount of the congregation, in the sides of the north: I will ascend above the heights of the clouds; I will be like the most High. (Isa. 14:12-14)

Other thrones, dominions, principalities and powers placed over other parts of the universe:

Who is the image of the invisible God, the firstborn of every creature: For by him were all things created, that are in heaven, and that

are in earth, visible and invisible, whether
they be thrones, or dominions, or principalities, or powers: all things were created by him,
and for him: And he is before all things, and
by him all things consist (Col. 1:15-17)

The Kingdom of God universal; God the Su-preme Moral Governor of the universe, and all in harmony with Him:

This matter is by the decree of the watchers,
and the demand by the word of the holy ones:
to the intent that the living may know that
the most High ruleth in the kingdom of men,
and giveth it to whomsoever he will, and
setteth up over it the basest of men. (Dan. 4:17)

Lucifer, the original ruler of the planet earth, conceives the idea that he can get the coopera-tion of other angelic beings of the universe, dethrone God, and become the exalted supreme ruler of the universe:

Thou sealest up the sum, full of wisdom, and
perfect in beauty. Thou hast been in Eden
the garden of God; every precious stone was
thy covering, the sardius, topaz, and the dia-
mond, the beryl, the onyx, and the jasper, the
sapphire, the emerald, and the carbuncle, and
gold: the workmanship of thy tabrets and of
thy pipes was prepared in thee in the day that
thou wast created. Thou art the anointed
cherub that covereth; and I have set thee so:
thou wast upon the holy mountain of God;
thou hast walked up and down in the midst
of the stones of fire. Thou wast perfect in thy
ways from the day that thou wast created, till

iniquity was found in thee. By the multitude
of thy merchandise they have filled the midst
of thee with violence, and thou hast sinned:
therefore I will cast thee as profane out of the
mountain of God: and I will destroy thee, O
covering cherub, from the midst of the stones
of fire. Thine heart was lifted up because of
thy beauty, thou hast corrupted thy wisdom
by reason of thy brightness: I will cast thee to
the ground, I will lay thee before kings, that
they may behold thee. (Ezek. 28:12b-17)

**Lucifer carries out his plans, and through pride
falls and incites rebellion by slander and accu-
sations against the Almighty. He causes his own
subjects and over one-third of God's angels to
rebel against Him. The earth enters its first sinful career:**

And his tail drew the third part of the stars of
heaven, and did cast them to the earth: and
the dragon stood before the woman which was
ready to be delivered, for to devour her child
as soon as it was born. (Rev. 12:4)

And there was war in heaven: Michael and
his angels fought against the dragon; and the
dragon fought and his angels, And prevailed
not; neither was their place found any more
in heaven. And the great dragon was cast out,
that old serpent, called the Devil, and Satan,
which deceiveth the whole world: he was cast
out into the earth, and his angels were cast
out with him. (Rev. 12:7-9)

Lucifer instigates rebellion and persuades oth-

ers to rebel. He openly breaks relations with God and His government, and leads his rebels from the appointed place of mobilization on earth into Heaven to dethrone God:

> How art thou fallen from heaven, O Lucifer, son of the morning! how art thou cut down to the ground, which didst weaken the nations! For thou hast said in thine heart, I will ascend into heaven, I will exalt my throne above the stars of God: I will sit also upon the mount of the congregation, in the sides of the north: I will ascend above the heights of the clouds; I will be like the most High. (Isa. 14:12-14)

Lucifer is met by Michael and the faithful angels, and is defeated and cast as lightning back to the earth:

> And there was war in heaven: Michael and his angels fought against the dragon; and the dragon fought and his angels, and prevailed not; neither was their place found any more in heaven. And the great dragon was cast out, that old serpent, called the Devil, and Satan, which deceiveth the whole world: he was cast out into the earth, and his angels were cast out with him. (Rev. 12:7-9)

God completely destroys Lucifer's kingdom and curses the earth by destroying all life. A great flood leaves the earth an empty wasteland:

> And the earth was without form, and void; and darkness was upon the face of the deep. And the Spirit of God moved upon the face of the waters. (Gen. 1:2; cf. Ezek. 28:11-19)

The Spirit of God begins to move upon the flooded earth and in the darkness which covered the waters to restore the earth to a habitable state, and to create new land animals, fish, fowls, vegetation, and Adam as the new ruler of the earth:

> Thou coveredst it with the deep as with a garment: the waters stood above the mountains. At thy rebuke they fled; at the voice of thy thunder they hasted away. They go up by the mountains; they go down by the valleys unto the place which thou hast founded for them. Thou hast set a bound that they may not pass over; that they turn not again to cover the earth. (Ps. 104:6-9)

Length of the re-creation is six days:

> Remember the sabbath day, to keep it holy. Six days shalt thou labour, and do all thy work: But the seventh day is the sabbath of the LORD thy God: in it thou shalt not do any work, thou, nor thy son, nor thy daughter, thy manservant, nor thy maidservant, nor thy cattle, nor thy stranger that is within thy gates: For in six days the LORD made heaven and earth, the sea, and all that in them is, and rested the seventh day: wherefore the LORD blessed the sabbath day, and hallowed it. (Ex. 20:8-11)

The earth is made perfect again and all things in the universe are in harmony with God as before Lucifer's rebellion; except Lucifer and his spirit rebels are still at large in the heavenlies:

> And you hath he quickened, who were dead

in trespasses and sins; Wherein in time past ye walked according to the course of this world, according to the prince of the power of the air, the spirit that now worketh in the children of disobedience: Among whom also we all had our conversation in times past in the lusts of our flesh, fulfilling the desires of the flesh and of the mind; and were by nature the children of wrath, even as others. (Eph. 2:1-3)

Lucifer (now the devil or adversary of God and man called Satan) enters the restored earth, tempts man and causes his fall, thus regaining dominion of the earth and all things therein: Now the serpent was more subtil than any beast of the field which the LORD God had made. And he said unto the woman, Yea, hath God said, Ye shall not eat of every tree of the garden? And the woman said unto the serpent, We may eat of the fruit of the trees of the garden: But of the fruit of the tree which is in the midst of the garden, God hath said, Ye shall not eat of it, neither shall ye touch it, lest ye die. And the serpent said unto the woman, Ye shall not surely die: For God doth know that in the day ye eat thereof, then your eyes shall be opened, and ye shall be as gods, knowing good and evil. And when the woman saw that the tree was good for food, and that it was pleasant to the eyes, and a tree to be desired to make one wise, she took of the fruit thereof, and did eat, and gave also unto her husband with her; and he did eat. (Gen. 3:1-6).

Rebellion starts again on the earth by the sec-

ond ruler of earth. Man is judged, the earth is again cursed and enters its second sinful career, and all creatures are brought under the bondage of sin and corruption:

> Wherefore, as by one man sin entered into the world, and death by sin; and so death passed upon all men, for that all have sinned. (Rom. 5:12)

"The heavens and the earth, which are now" since the restoration work of the six days, and since the new curse on the earth await the time of the second renovation, and the third perfect state of the earth called the new heavens and the new earth:

> And, thou, Lord, in the beginning hast laid the foundation of the earth; and the heavens are the works of thine hands: They shall perish; but thou remainest; and they all shall wax old as doth a garment; And as a vesture shalt thou fold them up, and they shall be changed: but thou art the same, and thy years shall not fail. (Heb. 1:10-12; cf. 2 Pet. 3:5-7)

Bibliography

Brown, Walt. *Is There a Large Gap of Time Between Genesis 1:1 and 1:2?* <http://www.creationscience.com/onlinebook/toc.html>. 28 Oct 1996.

Custance, Arthur C. *Without Form and Void.* Brockville, Ontario: Doorway Publications, 1970.

Dake, Finis J. *God's Plan For Man.* Lawrenceville, Georgia: Dake Bible Sales, Inc., 1987.

Dake, Finis J. *The Dake Annotated Reference Bible.* Lawrenceville, Georgia: Dake Bible Sales, Inc., 1991.

Howe, Frederic R. *The Age of the Earth: An Appraisal of Some Current Evangelical Positions.* <http://www.bible.org/bibsac/8594/85a3.htm#11>. 18 Nov 1996.

Morris, Henry M. *The Gap Theory an Idea With Holes?* <http://www.christiananswers.net/aig/cmadvert.html>. 5 Nov 1996.

Morris, Henry M. *The Revival of Modern Creationism.* <http://www.icr.org/pubs/btg/btg-080.htm>. 12 Dec 1996.

Nelson, Paul. *An Interview With Michael Denton.* <http://www.mrccos.com/arn/orpages/or152/dent.htm>. 28 Nov 1996.

Sharp, Doublas B. *Creation Models.* <http://www.sojourn.com/~revev/web/models.html>. 3 Nov 1996.

Stedman, Ray C. *Out of Darkness.* <http://www.pbc.org/dp/stedman/genesis/0302.html>. 3 Nov 1996.